PARTICIPANT WORKBOOK

The 6Ds Workshop

Roy V. H. Pollock

Andrew Jefferson

Calhoun W. Wick

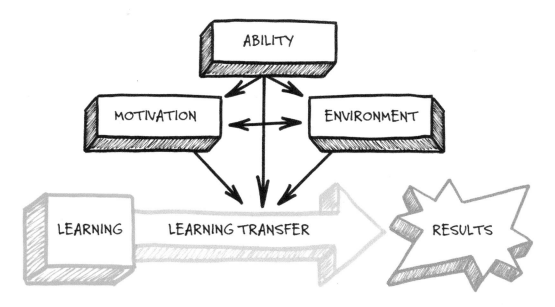

WILEY

ISBN: 978-1-118-64803-2
Acquiring Editor: Matthew Davis
Director of Development: Kathleen Dolan Davies
Production Editor: Dawn Kilgore
Editor: Rebecca Taff
Editorial Assistant: Ryan Noll
Manufacturing Supervisor: Becky Morgan
Illustrations by Ris Fleming-Allen
Illustrations © 2013, The 6Ds Company, unless otherwise noted.
Printed in the United States of America
Printing   10 9 8 7

Use of this workbook to teach the 6Ds® is prohibited without the express written permission from the 6Ds Company.

CONTENTS

Reading the 6Ds on Mt. Ararat, courtesy of Alban Le Nech

Welcome to the 6Ds® Workshop

The goal of this workshop is for you to apply 6Ds insights, tools, and practices so that you increase the value that training delivers to your organization.

The 6Ds Workshop is based on the best-selling book, *The Six Disciplines of Breakthrough Learning: How to Turn Training and Development into Business Results* (Wick, Pollock, & Jefferson, 2010). The 6Ds are the six practices that high-impact training organizations consistently apply in designing, delivering, and evaluating training programs.

Companies that have adopted the 6Ds earn a higher return on their training investments and enjoy a more productive working relationship between business and training professionals.

A core concept of the 6Ds is that converting learning into improved performance is a process, not an event. Therefore, training and development should embrace the tools, concepts, and proven value of process improvement methodology. Even if your training is already top-notch, applying the concepts from this workshop will help

"We are not in the business of providing classes, learning tools, or even learning itself. We are in the business of facilitating improved business results."

—Fred Harburg, CLO, Fidelity Investments

you increase its value to your organization and enhance your reputation as a strategic partner in the business.

The key is having the discipline to consistently apply the 6Ds. The concepts themselves are easy to understand; they are in many ways common sense. But they are not common practice. This workshop emphasizes practical application of the 6Ds to enhance the value of the important work you do. Checklists for each D, planners, and other job aids are provided.

Introduction

"Learning has the opportunity to be one of the most strategically aligned, well-planned, and well-executed functions in an organization."

—David Vance, *The Business of Learning*

Introduction

In today's competitive, knowledge-based business environment, both formal and informal learning are vital to staying competitive. Structured (formal or planned) learning is efficient for establishing baseline skills and knowledge, and essential to ensure consistency and universal exposure to key concepts and practices. Training professionals thus make a critical contribution toward achieving their organizations' goals, *provided the training they deliver is used on the job in a way that improves performance.*

The goal of this workshop is to have you apply the insights, tools, processes, and practices of the 6Ds so that:

❏ The training you design and deliver produces positive impact
❏ You enhance your reputation as a strategic business partner
❏ The training department is a highly valued and visible contributor to your organization's success

Even if your training is already excellent, there is always room for improvement. Applying the concepts from this workshop will

❏ Increase the value of training and development in your organization
❏ Enhance your reputation as a strategic partner in success

What Makes Learning Valuable?

Why This Exercise?

An overarching goal of this workshop is to enhance the value that training delivers to your organization. To do that, we need to be clear about what value means.

Instructions

1. Discuss the two topics below with your colleagues.
2. Generate several bullet points for each.
3. Be prepared to share with the group.

Think about the most valuable training you ever attended. Based on your personal experience, list the key characteristics that make learning valuable *from a participant's point of view:*

Now think about training from the organization's point of view. What are the characteristics of truly valuable learning *from a business leader's perspective?*

The Business We Are in

Organizations invest in training and development with the *expectation* that it will produce improved performance. (See Figure I.1.) That means:

1. Training's *product* is _Improve Performance_, not programs or modules; they are just the means to an end. Organizations "buy" training in the expectation of improved performance.

2. Our *value* to individuals and to the organization as a whole is the extent to which we help them _____ and meet their _____.

We will return to these key themes repeatedly throughout the workshop.

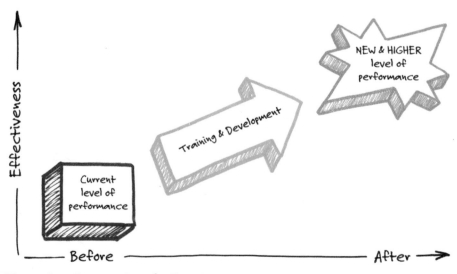

Figure I.1. Expectations for Training

Workshop Agenda

In keeping with the 6Ds principles, but unlike most training programs you have attended, this workshop does not end when the class ends. Instead, it is a two-month-long learning experience that began with pre-workshop learning and which will continue after we adjourn tomorrow, as seen in the timeline in Figure I.2. As we like to say, "The real work begins when the class ends." You will have "crossed the finish line" for this workshop when you can report successful application of the 6Ds principles to your work.

The agenda is as follows:

Days –20 to –1	Phase I, pre-workshop learning
Day 1 AM	Introduction and D1
Day 1 PM	D2 and D3
Day 2 AM	D4 and D5
Day 2 PM	D6, Goal Setting, Action Planning, and Feed Forward
Day 3 onward	Put learning to work
2 months	Share successes and lessons learned

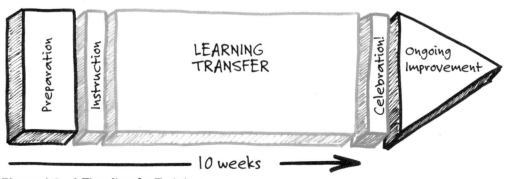

Figure I.2. A Timeline for Training

Getting Your Money's Worth

To get the full value of the investment that you and your organization are making in this workshop:

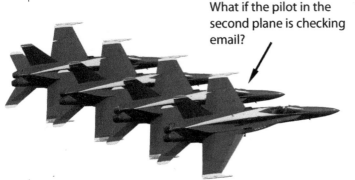

What if the pilot in the second plane is checking email?

❑ **Be present.** Research shows that when people attempt to multi-task during training, learning suffers. Please restrict email, texting, and phone use to breaks.

❑ **Participate.** Contribute to the activities and discussions. Your opinion matters and contributes to everyone's learning. Active participation enhances your own understanding and recall.

❑ **Ask questions.** Ask for clarification if you are not sure that you understand a point or if you want to know more about a topic or recommendation.

❑ **Challenge.** Speak up if you have a different opinion or different experience. Counter-examples enrich the discussion and understanding.

Meet Your Colleagues

The 6Ds Workshop is a shared learning journey. We will be working together in pairs and small groups throughout our time together. Please take a few minutes to introduce yourself to the people with whom you are seated. Briefly explain your role and the program you will be using as a case study during the activities.

Name	Role/Organization	Program

Training's Effectiveness Today

After any training program—regardless of the instructional method or medium—some participants are more successful at applying what they learned and improving their performance than others, as seen in Figure I.3.

Given that the ultimate goal of training is to improve performance, the question is: What is the effectiveness of training today?

Your Turn

Estimate Current Yield

Why This Exercise?

In any process improvement effort, it is important to establish a baseline. The purpose of this exercise is to discuss the effectiveness of typical training programs today as a way to gauge the magnitude of the opportunity for improvement.

Instructions

1. Discuss the question below with your colleagues.
2. Come to a consensus estimate.
3. Be prepared to share with the group; we will tabulate the results.

After a typical training program, what percent of participants use what they have learned well enough and long enough that they improve their performance?

Your estimate = _____%

Range of group's estimates = _____% to _____%

notes

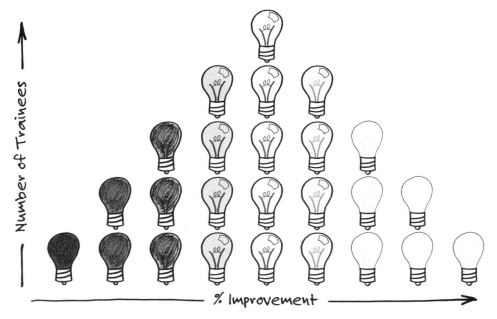

Figure I.3. Improvement After Training

Customer Satisfaction

A customer's satisfaction with a product or service depends on how well it meets his or her expectations. Organizations invest in training with the expectation that it will improve on-the-job performance. So if managers send employees to training, but on-the-job performance remains unchanged, they conclude that "the training failed." They are dissatisfied with their investment and consider it a waste of time and money.

As learning professionals, should we be concerned?

What Do You Think?

By your own estimates, training often fails to produce the performance improvement that management expected. But how serious a problem is this?

Talk to your colleagues and come up with an answer to this question:

In a survey conducted by the Executive Board, what percent of managers said that employee performance *would not change or would be improved if Learning and Development were eliminated today?*

Your group's estimate: _____
Research study findings: _____

The results should be a wake-up call to everyone in training and development. We need to do more to ensure that training produces the results that management wants and expects.

 ## Why Is So Much Training Scrap?

We coined the term "learning scrap" to describe training that employees attend, but then never apply in a way that improves their performance.

There are four main contributors to learning scrap:

1. When training is not the right solution
2. When the wrong people are trained or are trained at the wrong time

3. When the training itself is ineffective (poorly designed or executed)
4. When the learning is not transferred and reinforced on the job

Training Isn't Always the Solution

The right training at the right time for the right people can be a significant source of competitive advantage. But training is not a panacea. Training is an important part of the solution for some performance issues. But there are others that training will not resolve and, indeed, in which training could make the situation worse. Before we talk about creating more effective training, we need to be sure that training is warranted in the first place.

Your Turn

When Is Training the Right Solution?

Why This Exercise?

Unfortunately, many managers see training as the solution to every kind of management problem. The inappropriate use of training is a major contributor to learning scrap and training failures. Therefore, learning professionals must do a better job of helping managers understand when training will help resolve a performance issue and when it won't. This exercise explores the appropriate and inappropriate uses of training.

Instructions

1. Work with your colleagues to populate the chart on the next page.
2. Be prepared to share examples with the larger group.

Situations in which training is appropriate	Situations in which training will be a waste of time and money
Competitive landscape	When is redundant
New Indications or Product	Buss level or process it's Broken.
Specific need for a group of people.	
Brand new model	
New to organization	
New to process,	

notes

How to Handle Requests for Training

Respond Positively

When you receive a request for training—even if you strongly suspect that training is not an appropriate response—the first words out of your mouth should be: "_____" (Stolovitch & Keeps, 2004, p. 93).

Why? First, because your client called you asking for help. If you can lead him or her to a better solution—even one that does not ultimately involve training—then you have acted as a true performance consultant. You will have helped the client and the organization and avoided a lot of learning scrap.

By starting with a positive statement—"I can help you"—you position yourself as a strategic partner.

Explore Non-Training Solutions First

Bob Mager suggests that the most important single question in deciding whether or not training is warranted is:

> "If _____, would _____?" (*Analyzing Performance Problems*, p. 93).

He reasons that you won't improve performance by training people how to do something they already know how to do (Figure I.4). A flow chart to help you think through other causes of performance gaps is provided in the Appendix.

"Training is expensive to design and deliver; it should be the last, not the first, intervention the HRD professional and organization should consider."

—Broad and Newstrom, *Transfer of Training*

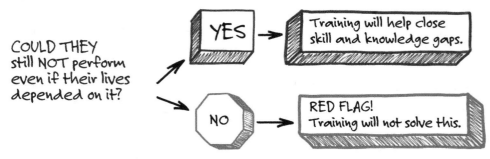

Figure I.4. To Train or Not to Train

What Do You Think?

When training fails to improve performance, managers often request re-training. In our experience, re-training almost never solves the problem. Why is that? Confer with your colleagues and suggest why re-training rarely works.

"If a genuine lack of skill is not the problem, then you can forget training as a potential solution."

—Bob Mager, *Analyzing Performance Problems*

notes

The Moment of Truth

At the end of the day, whether training adds value or becomes just more learning scrap comes down to what employees do at the "moment of truth."

The "moment of truth" is when a recently trained employee decides (consciously or unconsciously) how to perform a task or action (Figure I.5). He or she has two choices:

❏ To continue to do things as he or she did prior to training, or
❏ To do things in the new manner he or she was just taught.

Figure I.5. Choosing the New Way Over the Old

Doing things the "old way" is easy. It has the strong force of habit behind it. It is familiar and often automatic. Doing things a new way (transferring the training to the job) requires conscious thought and effort. It will probably take longer at first, and the employee will probably not be as proficient initially.

Which path an employee chooses depends on the answer to two fundamental questions (Figure I.6):

- 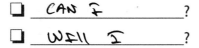 CAN I _____ ?
- WILL I _____ ?

An employee must answer *both* questions in the affirmative for the learning to be transferred and positively impact performance.

The answers to the "Can I?" and "Will I?" questions depend on the answers to seven underlying questions.

Figure I.6. Essential Questions

Fundamental Question	Underlying Questions
Can I?	- Did program actually teach me how? - Do I have the opportunity to do so? - Am I confident enough to try? - Can I get help if I need it?
Will I?	• Am I motivated enough to make the effort? • Am I convinced it will help me? • Will anybody notice I do? • What does my boss think? • What do my peers think.

Throughout the workshop, we will use the "Can I?"/"Will I?" questions as organizing principles to show that *everything* about the program design, delivery, and work environment—before as well as after training—affects whether or not training delivers on its promise.

Keep in mind that *both* "Can I?" and "Will I?" must be answered "yes" for performance to improve. Of the four possible combinations of answers, only one (when both are yes) creates value for the organization.

Answer to the "Can I?" question	Answer to "Will I?" Question	
	No	YES
YES	Learning Scrap	Value creation through learning transfer
No	Learning Scrap	Learning Scrap

BOTTOM LINE

To ensure that training delivers value, we as learning professionals need to learn to influence *all* of the factors that affect how learners answer the "Can I?" and "Will I?" questions.

The 6Ds and Instructional Design

The 6Ds (Figure I.7) are a mnemonic and model for thinking holistically and systematically about what it takes to transform training into business results. Organizations that enjoy the highest returns on their investments in training and development practice the 6Ds, which are

❑ **De**fine business outcomes.
❑ **De**sign the *complete* experience.
❑ **De**liver for application.
❑ **Dr**ive learning transfer.
❑ **De**ploy performance support.
❑ **Do**cument results.

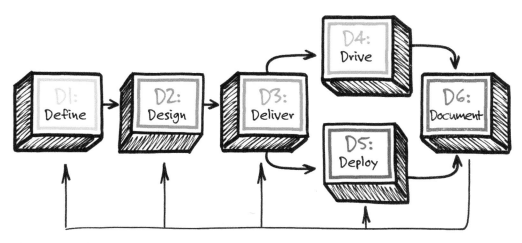

Figure I.7. The 6Ds

The 6Ds are an extension of traditional design models such as ADDIE, *not a replacement*. A sound instructional design methodology is essential for any training to be effective. But more than great instruction is needed to deliver business value.

Instructional design models focus on the period of instruction (class, e-learning module, etc.). What the 6Ds add is a much stronger focus on *business* outcomes. The 6Ds extend and complement ADDIE by emphasizing the need for planning and influencing the pre- and post-training environments by ensuring accountability, performance support, managerial engagement, and evaluation of on-the-job results (Figure I.8).

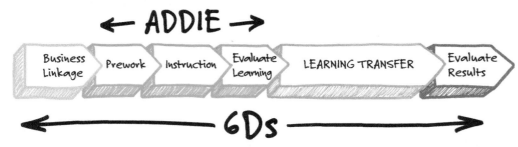

Figure I.8. The 6Ds Extend ADDIE

In the rest of the instructor-led portion of this workshop we will address each of the Ds in turn, showing how each is essential to achieving the overall goal of corporate training (improved performance) and how each discipline helps employees to answer the "Can I?" and "Will I" questions in the affirmative.

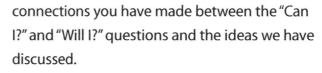

Reflect and Plan

Why This Exercise?

One of the key principles of *Forum's Principles of Workplace Learning* is that true learning requires alternating cycles of action and reflection. To help you maximize the value of this workshop, we will pause after each section to give you time to reflect, record your key takeaways, and consider actions you can take to put your learning to work.

Learning research has shown that the more and richer the number of mental connections to a concept (elaboration), the more durable and usable it becomes. We'll be using a concept called "mind mapping" to help you make mental connections. (See Greater Insight I.1.)

Instructions

1. Reflect on this introduction and your notes.

2. Use the Two Questions Mind Map (Figure A.2) in the Appendix to draw the connections you have made between the "Can I?" and "Will I?" questions and the ideas we have discussed.

3. Consider this question: "If the workshop were to end right now, what actions could I take to apply what I have learned so far that would help me and my organization?"

4. Jot a few ideas for action on the 6Ds Road Map to Results™ in the Appendix (Figure A.1). If you need suggestions, you can refer to the "Ideas into Action" job aid in the Appendix.

5. Contribute to the collective wisdom of the group. Transfer one or two of your best ideas to sticky notes and post them on the community maps on the wall.

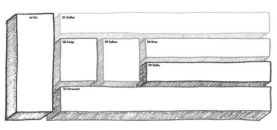

Figure A.1 Road Map to Results

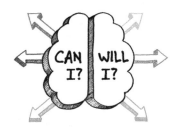

Figure A.2 Two Questions Mind Map.

GREATER INSIGHT I.1

Mind Maps

A *mind map* is a diagram that illustrates the connections among ideas. Mind maps are usually constructed around a central idea or concept. Core concepts are drawn as major trunks radiating out from the center; more detailed and supporting concepts are shown as branches, twigs, and leaves.

The purpose of creating a mind map is to make the relationships among concepts easier to remember. Brain research has shown that images are stored separately from words. The two memory systems complement one another and help boost recall. For this reason, proponents of mind maps recommend using colors and pictures or sketches—rather than just words—to create more memorable images.

Mind maps were popularized by Tony Buzan (*The Mind Map Book*) as a way to enhance memory and understanding. He proposed a number of "laws" of mind mapping that include:

1. Use emphasis:
   a. Use images.
   b. Use at least three colors.
   c. Vary the size of lines, images, and printing to show importance.
   d. Make use of spacing.
2. Use association:
   a. Draw arrows to make connections across branches.
   b. Use colors to show relatedness among similar ideas.
3. Be clear:
   a. Print.
   b. Connect lines.
   c. Make the central lines thicker.
4. Develop a personal style:
   a. Figure out what works best for you.
5. Use hierarchy.
6. Use numerical order.

There are many examples of mind maps on the Internet. Mind-mapping software is even available commercially.

Research results on the value of drawing mind maps is mixed, although the underlying principle is well established by learning research: the more elaborate the neural connections to a concept, the easier it is to recall.

Many people find mind maps a useful way to take notes. We include it in this workshop to help you summarize the key concepts from each section and so you can decide its value for you personally.

SUMMING UP

- From the organization's point of view, great training improves performance and contributes to achieving the organization's mission and goals.

- From a participant's point of view, great training is relevant, practical, and immediately applicable. It is engaging and builds on what participants already know.

- In most organizations today, a significant amount of training is never used; it goes to waste and adds to the learning scrap heap.

- There are numerous causes of learning scrap, but the two most common are using training for the wrong reasons and providing inadequate support for learning transfer.

- A critical "moment of truth" occurs back on the job after training when employees make the decision to perform in the way they just learned or in the way they always have.

- The answers to two fundamental questions—"Can I?" and "Will I?"— determine whether training is used or goes to waste.

- *Everything* about the work environment, as well as the design, delivery, and support for training, affects the answers to the "Can I?" and "Will I?" questions.

- The 6Ds are a way to think holistically and systematically about the factors that affect training outcomes.

D1 Define Business Outcomes

"The only reason that learning functions exist is to drive business outcomes."

—Rita Smith, *Strategic Learning Alignment*

Order-Takers Versus Trusted Advisors

Who do you think is paid more: an order-taker at a fast-food restaurant or a trusted advisor like a physician, attorney, or financial advisor? For learning professionals to be respected as true professionals and trusted advisors, we have to do more than just take orders and serve up training.

Your Turn

What's the Difference?

Why This Exercise?

The purpose of this exercise is to contrast the characteristics of order-takers to those of trusted advisors. The goal is to identify what we need to do to become more highly valued and better appreciated.

Instructions

1. For each of the attributes below, check which characterize order-takers, and which describe trusted advisors and strategic business partners. (Some apply to both.)

Attribute	Order-Taker	Trusted Advisor
Has in-depth knowledge of instructional design and delivery principles.		

Promptly and efficiently delivers the requested training.		
Accepts the sponsor's analysis of the issue since they know the business.		
Probes for understanding of the underlying business issues.		
Completes a task- and needs-assessment only *after* the business goals are clear.		
Pushes back when training is not the right solution and proposes non-training alternatives.		
Can explain how the company makes money and the key challenges that the business faces.		
Matches the training to the required job performance.		
Waits to be asked to deliver training solutions.		
Proactively suggests where training can help meet business challenges.		
Measures and reports learners' reactions; revises training as needed to improve low scores.		
Measures and reports on-the-job behaviors and results; revises training as necessary to improve low scores.		
Proactively recommends removing or revising courses that are no longer high priority.		
"Sells" the value of training to the organization.		

2. Compare your ratings with those of your colleagues.

3. Then discuss the implications for training professionals. Complete the chart below. What do we need to do more of, and what do we need to do less of, to become more valuable and more highly regarded partners in the success of our organizations?

To become more of a trusted business advisor, learning professionals need to:

Do more:	
Do less:	

4. Be prepared to share your ratings and the implications with the larger group.

5. Use these insights to create one personal goal for yourself.

One thing I can do personally to increase my value is

BOTTOM LINE

Learning professionals can increase their value and the respect they command by consciously striving to become trusted advisors to their business partners. To do so requires an understanding of the business and a genuine focus on the client's needs in addition to expertise in training design and delivery. (See Greater Insight D1.1.)

"Expected credibility is what you know about your solution. Exceptional credibility is what you know about your customer and his or her business."

—Jeff Thull, *Mastering the Complex Sale*

GREATER INSIGHT D1.1

What Makes a Trusted Advisor?

In their book, *The Trusted Advisor,* Maister, Green, and Galford (2000) include the following as key characteristics of trusted advisors. They:

1. Focus on the client rather than themselves.
2. Treat clients as individuals rather than "roles."
3. Believe that problem definition and resolution are more important than technical or content mastery.
4. Are driven to constantly find new ways to be of greater service to their clients.
5. Focus on doing the right thing rather than on organizational politics.
6. View methodologies, models, and techniques only as a means to an end; they should be used only when they will be effective for *this* client.
7. Understand that both serving and selling are aspects of professionalism; both are concerned with proving to clients that you can help them with their issues.

How Do Training and Development Add Value?

Training is an investment; it takes time and it costs money. It must create value greater than its cost and comparable to other investments of similar magnitude.

Whether you work in a for-profit corporation or a not-for-profit enterprise or government agency, the math is simple: *an organization must bring in at least as much money as it pays out in expenses.*

Therefore, at the highest level of generalization, there are only two ways that training can contribute to success (Figure D1.1):

- ☐ Increased the income
- ☐ Decreased in cost

That is not to say that there are not also morally defensible and socially valuable benefits to training, but in a corporate enterprise, training must first and foremost contribute to organizational survival and profitability.

Figure D1.1. The Two Ways Training Contributes to Success

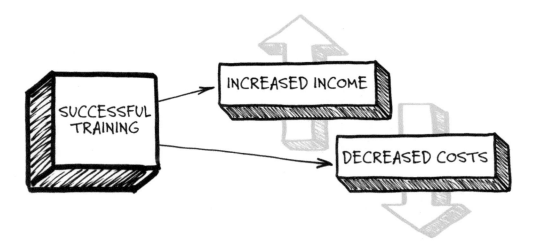

Your Turn

"Every business
is the same
inside."

—Ram Charan,
*What the CEO
Wants You to Know*

Provide Examples

Why This Exercise?

To be valued as strategic partners in the organization's success, we need to be able to explain how what we do contributes to its mission and goals. The purpose of this exercise is to think through how different kinds of training programs contribute to your organization's success.

Instructions

In the first row of the chart below, we have listed a few general examples of how organizations can increase revenues and decrease costs.

1. Add several examples specific to your organization.
2. Come up with an example of a training program you have today that helps increase revenue and one that helps reduce (or avoid) costs.
3. Explain how the program helps achieve the goal. For example, a program on compliance should reduce the potential risk and attendant costs of a regulatory or legal action.
4. Finally, note any program that doesn't seem to fit in either pathway.

Goal	Increase Revenue	Decrease Costs
General Examples	Improve salespeople's productivity Enhance customer satisfaction Improve product quality	Reduce number of injuries Improve employee retention Increase efficiency of a process

Goal	Increase Revenue	Decrease Costs
Specific examples for our organization		
A training program in our organization		
How it helps achieve our goals		

A program (if any) that I do not think serves either purpose is _____

_____

Why? _____

_____

Features Versus Benefits

One of the basic skills that new salespeople need to master is to distinguish between features and benefits. They need to be able to explain how the product will *benefit* the customer, rather than just enumerating its attributes.

What Do You Think?

One feature of a particular automobile might be: "A one-piece, reinforced, heavy-gauge, welded steel frame."

How would you describe its advantages compared to, say, "A cheap, tinny frame that is bolted together from a lot of pieces"? _____

_____

_____

_____

_____

Therefore, how would you explain the *benefits* of the one-piece frame to a potential car buyer?

_____

_____

_____

In general, what is the difference between a feature and a benefit? The difference is that features are _____ , whereas benefits _____ .

The distinction is important because people buy *expected benefits, not features per se.*

Application to Training and Development

We raise the distinction between features and benefits here because the vast majority of descriptions of training programs describe their *features* without ever clearly stating the benefits to the participants and company.

notes

Describe the Benefits of Your Program

Why This Exercise?

Managers will be more willing to invest in training if we do a better job of explaining its *benefits*. One way to help clarify the benefits is the FAB approach: making a table of the Features, their Advantages, and the resulting Benefits.* This exercise is an opportunity to apply this method to your own program.

Instructions

1. Review the example.
2. Then, using a program of your own, list several of its features in the left-hand column.
3. In the center column, list the advantages of this feature.
4. Finally, in the third column, list the *benefits for the participants and the organization*.
5. Help each other.
6. Be prepared to share insights or challenges with the group.

*Thanks to Don Ledbetter of L3 Communications for teaching us this approach, which was originally developed by Neil Rackham in *SPIN Selling*.

Examples

Feature	Advantages	Benefits
Delivered virtually	No travel required	Lower cost and less time away from daily tasks
Lots of guided practice	Better learning than passively watching PowerPoint slides	New hires get up to speed more quickly Requires less supervisor time
Based on proven practices in our company	We know they work in our business More relevant than generic methods	Employees will achieve better results when they apply the methods taught in this class

Your Program

Feature	Advantages	Benefits

"If you think education is expensive, try ignorance."

—Derek Bok, Former President, Harvard University

Stake Your Claim

Why This Exercise?

Products make promises. They claim they will help you lose weight, save money, get through the airport faster, enjoy your weekend more, and so on and so on. The promise is the product's claim or *value proposition*. It answers the question: "Why should I buy this product or service?"

Training also makes promises. When you agree to conduct training, you make a promise—implicitly or explicitly—that the training will improve something. The purpose of this exercise is to help you learn to state the claim (promise, value proposition) of your program clearly and persuasively.

The claim calls out the most valuable and distinctive benefit and states it succinctly and boldly. Understanding a program's claim is vital to marketing its value and, as we will discuss when we discuss D6, to evaluating it.

Instructions

1. Review the ads provided.
2. What is the core claim or promise of each?

   a. ___"You will effectively Present the new ~~stix~~ for E"___

   b._____

3. Now try to write a claim for your program by completing the sentence below. Less is more; try to state your claim in twenty-five or fewer words.

   Can you dif the product in a crowden market.

   By applying what you learn in this course to your work, you will. . .

Learning Objectives Versus Business Outcomes

 ### What Do You Think?

True or False: You should always start a training program by listing the learning objectives.

Why or why not? _____

_____

Anyone familiar with instructional design knows that well-defined learning objectives are vital to guide training design. However, while learning objectives are important to indicate what needs to be taught, they are more like features than benefits. They do a poor job of communicating the *benefits of the training to participants and their managers*. They explain *what* will be learned, but not *why*. For that, you need to articulate the *business outcomes.*

The Distinction

Business outcomes differ from learning outcomes in two important dimensions: their time frame and focus:

	Traditional Learning Objectives	Business Outcome Objectives
Time frame	End of class	on the Job
Focus	Knowledge or capability.	Action and Result

Check for Understanding

Why This Exercise?

Differentiating between learning objectives and business outcome objectives is a prerequisite to becoming a trusted business partner. This exercise gives you a chance to test your understanding of the difference before we move on to its application.

Instructions

Indicate whether each of the following objectives describes a learning outcome (L) or a business outcome (B).

Ⓛ	B	After attending this program, the participant will be able to correctly define 100 percent of the steps in the Six Sigma DMADDI process and give an example of how each could be used to improve quality or reduce waste.
L	Ⓑ	By applying the Six Sigma principles taught in this course, the attendee will reduce waste in a selected business process by 5 percent within three months.
L	B	After completing this module, the attendee will correctly identify at least 80 percent of the most common errors made when giving feedback and be able to point out all six elements of constructive feedback during role plays.
L	B	Using the methods learned in this course, participants will provide more timely and more constructive feedback to their direct reports and improve their departments' engagement scores on the next employee survey by 10 percent or more.
L	B	By the end of this course, the attendees will be able to correctly reframe 90 percent of customers' potential objections during mock sales calls with their managers.
L	B	The attendee will improve sales close rates by 4 percent within three months by using the methods taught in this course to more effectively handle objections.

Strengths and Weaknesses

The relative strengths and weaknesses of defining learning versus business outcomes are summarized below.

	Advantages	Disadvantages
Learning objectives	Clearly communicate to instructional designers what learners must be able to do as a result of instruction. Suggest appropriate testing strategies to ensure that the material and skills were learned.	Do a poor job of explaining the benefits to the participants or to the business. Are usually formulaic and often full of learning jargon. A program can achieve all its learning objectives and still produce no tangible business value.
Business outcomes objectives	Clearly communicate the value to the organization and the what's-in-it-for-me (WIIFM) to the participants. Suggest the appropriate measures for assessing whether the program is producing the expected results. Achievement depends on factors outside the control of training and development.	Are not sufficiently detailed to guide instructional design. Achievement depends on factors outside the control of training and development.

BOTTOM LINE

❏ Both learning objectives and business outcomes objectives are required to effectively design and sell training, but they have different purposes.

❏ Learning objectives should be used for communication and planning among learning professionals.

❏ Business outcomes objectives should be used to communicate training's benefits to sponsors and participants.

❏ Business objectives should be defined first; learning objectives exist only to facilitate achievement of business goals.

Page 48 6th book.

"Objectives for learning and development should be developed at higher levels than traditional learning objectives."

—Elkeles and Phillips, *The Chief Learning Officer*

Defining Business Outcomes

Where do the business outcomes come from? How do you discover where training can add the greatest value?

What Do You Think?

The three most important goals for this year of the unit I support are

1. _Knowledge_

2. _~~Attraction~~ Effective pull though_

3. _____

   Were you able to complete the statement above? Are you confident about your answers? If not, you have identified an opportunity to improve your value.

> "Wherever there is a need, there is an opportunity."
>
> —Philip Kotler, *Kotler on Marketing*

notes

Know Your Business

To be a trusted advisor, you have to truly understand the goals of the organization you support. Can you answer the questions in the Self-Test of Business Knowledge (Greater Insight D1.2)? It's important that you be able to; such insights are critical to maximizing your contribution.

You don't need an MBA to be a great business partner, however; there are plenty of opportunities on the job to learn what you need to know. All it takes is a willingness to learn and a genuine interest in the challenges and opportunities your business partners are trying to manage.

Ideas into Action

- ❏ Deepen your understanding of the business you support.
- ❏ Read the business or operating plans.
- ❏ Attend business and operational reviews.
- ❏ Ask questions if you do not understand terms or concepts.
- ❏ Look for ways in which training and development can help address business issues.

GREATER INSIGHT D1.2

Self-Test of Business Knowledge

Plastipak Academy received Corporate University Xchange's Exemplary Practice Award for Business Alignment. According to Academy Leader Diane Hinton, "Plastipak Academy's success is built on our reputation as a business function that drives real business results through targeted learning solutions. We talk about business issues with leaders, not just in the context of learning and development. And we emphasize collaboration throughout the learning development and implementation process, leveraging leader involvement and learning transfer to achieve business results" (Quoted in Wick, Pollock, & Jefferson, 2010, p. 32).

Test yourself. Can you confidently answer the questions below? If so, congratulations, you are in touch with your business. If not, or if you struggled with some of the questions, then you have the opportunity to improve your performance by deepening your understanding of your organization's business.

1. The most important source of our revenue is . . .

2. The most important driver of our growth is . . .

3. The core elements of our strategy are (list) . . .

4. Our main competitor is . . .

5. The greatest threat we face is . . .

6. The greatest human capital challenge we face as a company is . . .

Getting Specific

How do you move from a general understanding of business goals and challenges to defining the objectives for a specific training initiative? You have to talk to the business leaders. They are the ones who know what they need to accomplish and who will decide whether the training did, or did not, meet their needs.

The Outcomes Planning Wheel

The 6Ds Outcomes Planning Wheel™ is a job aid that has proven very useful across a wide range of organizations and training needs (Figure D1.2). The questions on the planning wheel help business leaders articulate what they really want and how they will decide whether the training was a success or not. A discussion using the planning wheel should precede more detailed analysis. It will help you avoid "seeing the trees, but missing the forest."

Figure D1.2. The 6Ds Outcomes Planning Wheel™

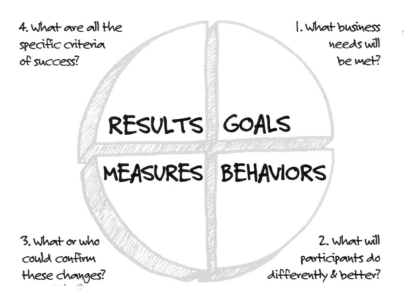

4. What are all the specific criteria of success?

1. What business needs will be met?

RESULTS | GOALS

MEASURES | BEHAVIORS

3. What or who could confirm these changes?

2. What will participants do differently & better?

D1 DEFINE BUSINESS OUTCOMES

Your Turn

Test Drive the Planning Wheel

Why This Exercise?

To give you an opportunity to practice using the planning wheel so you are prepared to use it effectively in your work with business leaders.

Instructions

1. Complete a planning wheel for your program (we will be using the results in later exercises).
2. Help each other and/or ask the facilitator for assistance.
3. Refer to the completed example (Figure D1.3) and to the job aid for using the planning wheel in the Appendix.
4. Be prepared to share insights or the challenges you foresee in using the planning wheel.

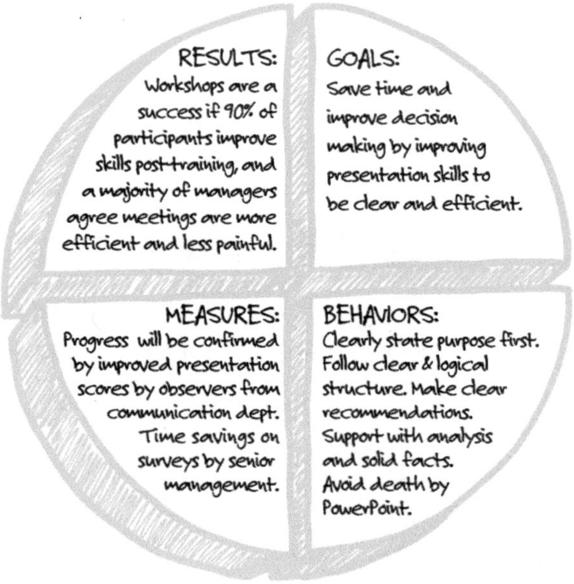
RESULTS:
Workshops are a success if 90% of participants improve skills post-training, and a majority of managers agree meetings are more efficient and less painful.
GOALS:
Save time and improve decision making by improving presentation skills to be clear and efficient.
MEASURES:
Progress will be confirmed by improved presentation scores by observers from communication dept. Time savings on surveys by senior management.
BEHAVIORS:
Clearly state purpose first. Follow clear & logical structure. Make clear recommendations. Support with analysis and solid facts. Avoid death by PowerPoint.

Figure D1.3. Completed Planning Wheel

Create Co-Ownership

A fifth question is a crucial part of the planning process: "If we want to ensure these behaviors on the job, **what else has to be in place?**" (Figure D1.4)

Figure D1.4. What Else?

After you have covered the four questions on the planning wheel itself, ask the manager to help you think through what else will be required to guarantee that employees will take the actions identified in Quadrant 2.

Explain that you mean things in the post-training work environment, such as support from managers, reinforcing rewards and recognition, consequences for non-compliance, and so forth. These are essential to improve on-the-job performance, but they are the purview of management and outside training and development's control.

Be sure to ask about how the trainees are evaluated and compensated. If the performance evaluation or compensation system rewards behaviors that are incompatible with those taught in training, then the training will fail to change behavior.

Be sure to write up the results of your discussion and send them to the business sponsor, either as an informal memo (like the sample in Figure D1.5) or as a formal contract between the learning organization and the business unit.

> "If you pit a good employee against a bad system, the system will win almost every time."
>
> —Geary Rummler

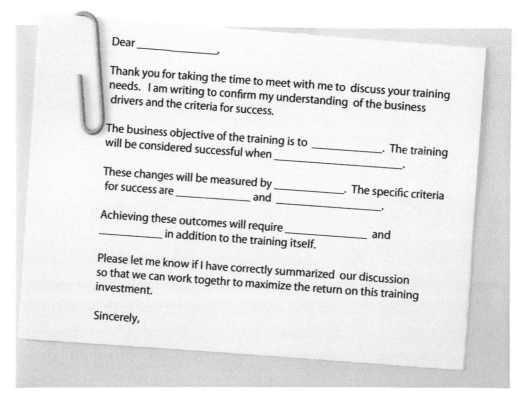

Dear _____,

Thank you for taking the time to meet with me to discuss your training needs. I am writing to confirm my understanding of the business drivers and the criteria for success.

The business objective of the training is to _____. The training will be considered successful when _____.

These changes will be measured by _____. The specific criteria for success are _____ and _____.

Achieving these outcomes will require _____ and _____ in addition to the training itself.

Please let me know if I have correctly summarized our discussion so that we can work togethr to maximize the return on this training investment.

Sincerely,

Figure D1.5. Sample Memo to the Business Sponsor

Ideas into Action

❏ Interview the business sponsor for a new or existing program using the Outcomes Planning Wheel.

❏ Triangulate the results with other stakeholders if appropriate.

❏ Summarize your findings and share with the key stakeholders.

❏ Review the incentive and performance review systems; if they are incompatible with the training, the training will fail. Call this to management's attention.

D1 Is the *Sine Qua Non* of Effective Training

We can't overemphasize the importance of D1. If you aren't clear about the business outcomes the organization is looking for from training, then you won't know where you are going or whether you ever got there. And you won't be of much value to the organization as a result.

D1 is the bedrock on which training success rests. *If you do not get D1 right, you cannot compensate by clever design, innovative technology, or brilliant facilitation.* You cannot be a valued business partner if you don't know the business requirements. Make it a point—some organizations make it mandatory—to have a clear statement of business purpose before you begin any other design or planning work.

"If you don't know where you are going, you won't know when you get there."

Reflect and Plan

Why This Exercise?

This exercise makes use of the well-established learning principle of "elaborative encoding": the more links you form to new knowledge, the easier it is to recall and use later. It also builds on the truism that if people set goals and make plans to do something, they are more likely to do them.

Instructions

1. Look back over this section and your notes.
2. Begin to fill out the 6Ds Mind Map (Figure A.3 in the Appendix) by adding in some key ideas and "twigs" to the D1 branch.
3. Extend your Two Questions Mind Map by adding any associations that come to mind between D1 and "Can I?" and "Will I?"
4. Reflect on this question: "What actions can I take to apply what I have learned about D1 that will help me and my organization?"
5. Jot a few ideas for action on your 6Ds Road Map to Results. If you need suggestions, you can refer to the "Ideas into Action" job aid in the Appendix.
6. Transfer one or two of your best ideas from your personal maps to sticky notes and post them on the community maps on the wall.
7. Take a minute to learn from your colleagues' ideas.

SUMMING UP

- Training creates value by helping organizations gather more resources (increase revenues) or make more efficient use of resources (decrease costs).

- Management expects training to result in improved performance.

- Trusted advisors are experts in their own fields who also truly understand and care about their clients' needs and goals.

- Training and Development needs to do a better job of communicating the *benefits* of training, not just its *features*.

- Learning objectives are essential to inform instructional design, but they are inadequate to communicate the value of training.

- The 6Ds Planning Wheel™ helps you get "the big picture" about the real goals of the business and the "conditions of satisfaction" of the sponsor.

- It is essential to help management understand that they are co-responsible for whether or not training ultimately achieves the desired business results.

6Ds

D2 Design the Complete Experience

"If you can't describe what you are doing as a process, you probably don't know what you are doing."

—J. Edwards Deming

Learning as Process

A process is defined as "a systematic series of actions directed toward some end" (*American College Dictionary*). Improving performance through training and development, then, is a *process*, not an event. It involves three major steps (Figure D2.1):

1. Learn new skills
2. Transfer them to the job
3. Improve performance by continued practice

In any process, there are inputs, operations (procedures), and outputs (Figure D2.2). The quality of the output depends on both the quality of the input as well as the way in which the operations are performed. The quality revolution began with the realization that any process could be broken into its components and studied. Once the process was understood, the output could be "continuously and forever" improved.

Figure D2.1. The Learning Process

Figure D2.2. Process Steps

While Total Quality Management, Kaizen, and later, Six Sigma, all have their origins in manufacturing, the principles can be applied to any business process—including training and development—to increase the quality of the output and decrease the cost of production. D2 is about treating learning as a process, identifying the key factors that impact the quality of the output (improved performance on the job), and working to improve them. Of course, developing people will always be less predictable than producing widgets; nevertheless, where process improvement methodologies have been applied to training and development, the results have been impressive (Islam, 2006, p. 187).

Learn by Analogy

Why This Exercise?

In teaching new concepts, it is helpful to start with a simple, familiar example on which to build new understanding. In this exercise, you are asked to analyze a seemingly straightforward example to draw some important parallels about what determines training's effectiveness.

Your Turn

Instructions

1. Read the scenario below.

   You have been asked to bring the cake for a birthday party for a colleague at work. The process is pretty straightforward:

   a. Buy a cake mix.

   b. Add egg and water.

   c. Bake.

   d. Cover with icing.

2. Jot down all the factors that affect whether the process results in a successful outcome.

3. Be prepared to discuss.

Factors That Affect the Success or Failure of Baking a Cake	
Input Factors	**Operational/Procedural Factors**

You control the

Your Turn

Application to Training and Development

The key point is that, whether you are running a manufacturing plant, baking a cake, or trying to improve performance through training, many factors influence the quality of the ultimate result.

In human resource development, it is helpful to think of these factors in three groups: those that occur before training, those that occur during training, and those that occur after training.

Brainstorm Influencers

Why This Exercise?

What happens before and after training has an impact on how much is learned and how much is ultimately transferred to work. In practice, most instructional design models, like ADDIE, focus almost exclusively on the training itself. Yet, when you apply process thinking, it is evident that many opportunities for improvement are outside the traditional boundaries of instructional design. This exercise is a chance to brainstorm *all* the factors that impact whether or not training leads to performance improvement. The goal is to expand the repertoire of things we do to improve results.

Instructions

1. With your colleagues, brainstorm the most important factors that influence the outcomes of training in three time periods: before, during, and after.
2. Jot them down in the chart on the next page.
3. Be prepared to share your ideas.

Factors That Affect the Success or Failure of Training to Improve Performance		
Before	**During**	**After**

Expectations Matter

 ### What Do You Think?

If we were to spin a roulette wheel, ask you to write down the number it landed on, and then ask you to estimate the percent of African countries in the United Nations, would the roulette wheel have any influence on your estimate?

My answer: ❑ Yes   ❑ No

What the research showed: _____

_____

_____

Priming Effects

Numerous studies in learning and human psychology have illustrated that people's expectations strongly influence their actual experience. A couple of examples:

Study	Differences in Expectations	How They Affected Outcome

notes

Application to Learning and Development

The attitudes that participants bring to training affect their experience, how much they learn, and how much they apply.

There is an element of self-fulfilling prophecy: learners who arrive with a bad attitude are less receptive to new ideas and approaches, less willing to participate in exercises, and less motivated to answer "Yes" to the "Will I?" question after class. The inverse is true for learners who arrive with a positive attitude. Thus, participants' coming-in attitudes have a significant influence on the eventual outcome, just as the quality of raw materials impacts the ultimate quality of manufacturing.

Participants in a training program generally fall into one of three groups:

1. _____ ("I am just here to serve my time.")
2. _____ ("This will be a nice break from real work.")
3. _____ ("I am interested in learning something new.")

The challenge for designers and trainers is to convert the prisoners and vacationers into explorers.* To succeed, that process needs to begin *before* class, with the course description or invitation. That's usually the first opportunity the training department has to "sell" the program and create positive "learning intentionality." Unfortunately, most invitations to corporate training sound more like a jury summons than an exciting opportunity to learn and grow.

*Thanks to Terrence Donahue , corporate director of training at Emerson, for sharing this insight.

Improve Your Course Description/Invitation

Why This Exercise?

This exercise is an opportunity to practice rewriting your course description or invitation to create a more positive attitude ("eager want") and greater learning intentionality. Keller's ARCS model posits four contributors to the motivation to learn: attention (A), relevance (R), confidence (C), and satisfaction (S) (Keller, 1999). Try to include at least three.

Instructions

1. Write an invitation to attend your program (or a course description if you prefer) that will make people enthusiastic about attending.
2. Stress the benefits rather than the features.
3. Put the most compelling statement up-front. ("Don't bury the lead," as they say in journalism.)
4. Exchange with a colleague and help each other.
5. Be prepared to share with the larger group.

Here is a compelling description/invitation to my program:

Ideas into Action

- ❏ Review your course descriptions and invitations.
- ❏ Rewrite them to clearly state the benefits and the value proposition.
- ❏ Test them on prospective attendees and managers.

Four Phases of the Learning-to-Improvement Process

It is helpful to think of the learning-to-improvement process in four phases (Figure D2.3).

- ❏ **Phase I: Preparation**. The assignments, background knowledge, and work experiences necessary to fully comprehend and benefit from the training.
- ❏ **Phase II: Instruction.** The formally planned period of instruction, which might be delivered live, virtually, as asynchronous e-learning, or through any of a number of other vehicles.
- ❏ **Phase III: Transfer.** The process of applying the instruction in the work environment and practicing to gain proficiency. Informal learning and coaching are key.
- ❏ **Phase IV: Achievement**. The "finish line" for any given training cycle or initiative is when people have achieved the desired performance improvement and are recognized for it.

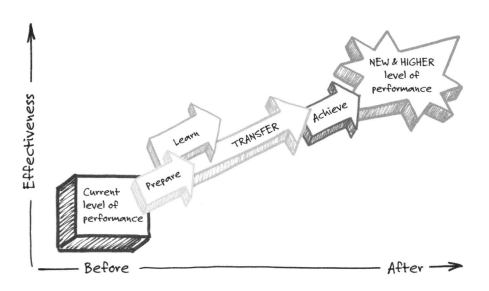

Figure D2.3. Four Phases of the Learning-to-Improvement Process

Preparation

The better prepared the participants are when the instruction begins, the more likely they are to benefit. Although many programs assign pre-work, participants often don't do it because it is seldom fully integrated into the program. Phase I learning should have a clear purpose and method appropriate to that purpose. The amount needs to be proportional to the importance of the training and realistic in terms of the time participants have to prepare.

 What Do You Think?

Table D2.1 lists the most common purposes for preparatory work. Review it and add creative examples that you have used or seen. Are there any other reasons for making assignments before training that should be added to the table?

Table D2.1. Purposes for Pre-Work

Purpose	Examples
Establish foundation knowledge; be sure all learners are "on the same page"	Reading short, targeted selections Completing an introductory e-learning program Having prerequisites, such as successful completion of a foundation course or specific work experiences
Stimulate interest in the topic	Experiential learning, such as interviewing a customer, patient, or senior leader; visiting a plant or office; listening to customer calls; and so forth Reading a provocative article or watching a video selected to provoke discussion Writing a short description of your own best/worst experience with something of relevance to the program
Create learning intentionality	A pre-training discussion between the manager and participant about what is most important Requiring a "learning contract" signed by both manager and participant Holding a pre-training teleconference that both managers and participants attend Giving a pre-training assessment to identify opportunities for improvement
Provide input to be used in the training	Having each participant bring a real and current issue to work on during the instruction Collecting 360-degree (or other) feedback on current performance Having all participants find and bring relevant examples from their work
Other: _____	_____ _____

Ideas into Action

- ❑ Review the pre-work you currently require. Is it essential to understand the instruction? Is the amount reasonable? Does it truly add value for the time required?
- ❑ Interview recent trainees. Did they do the pre-work? If not, why not? If they did, did it add value to the overall learning experience?
- ❑ Take action to address any issues you discover.

Managers Matter Before Training

One of the key factors that influences the answer to the "Will I?" question is "What does my boss think?" A learner's direct supervisor has a profound impact before, during, and after training. (See Greater Insight D2.1.)

GREATER INSIGHT D2.1

The Impact of Managers Before Training

Managers' actions (or inaction) prior to training influence learners' attitudes and, ultimately, whether or not they transfer what they learn to their work. For example, when Broad and Newstrom polled learning professionals about which time-role combination had the greatest impact on learning transfer, trainers rated the manager's involvement *prior* to the course as the single most powerful influence on whether the training ultimately would be transferred and applied (1992, p. 54).

This perception has been confirmed by many others. For example, Brinkerhoff and Montesino (1995) found that participants who had discussions with their managers before and after training reported significantly higher levels of skill application and felt more accountable for applying their learning.

Likewise, when Feldstein and Boothman (1997) compared high- and low-performance learners, they found that half of the factors that characterized high-performance learners were related to the influence of the manager. In a follow-up study, they implemented a system to increase the pre- and post-training interaction between learners and their managers. The result was that both the learners and their managers reported much higher rates of transfer.

Similarly, a study at American Express found that "high improvement" learners were four times more likely to have had a one-on-one conversation with their managers than the "no improvement" group (American Express, 2007). The bottom line is that managers directly impact the outcome of training—and that that influence begins before the training itself.

What Do You Think?

When do you think managers have the greatest influence on learning transfer?

- ❏ Before training
- ❏ During training
- ❏ After training

Don Kirkpatrick, in his classic work *Evaluating Training Programs: The Four Levels,* suggested that managers' reactions to training and development fell along a continuum, from very negative (actually forbidding or preventing participants from using what they learned) to very positive (requiring that they do). "Neutral" was the midpoint (see Figure D2.4).

Figure D2.4. Continuum of Reactions to Training and Development

notes

What Do You Think?

If a manager is "neutral," that is, says nothing one way or the other about the training that an employee is about attend, is that:

❏ Positive

❏ Neutral

❏ Negative

Why?

> notes

"The direct bosses of the training participants [are] absolutely critical to success."

—Mooney and Brinkerhoff, *Courageous Training*

Managers have a strong impact on the attitude with which participants approach training. When a manager complains about the "time away from work" or says nothing one way or the other, trainees conclude it is not important.

Conversely, managers have a strong positive effect when they have a pre-training discussion with their direct reports (see Greater Insight D2.2). These pre-training conversations need not be long or complicated. Merely showing an interest can be enough to tip the balance in favor of an active intent to learn. You can increase training's effectiveness by encouraging these discussions.

Ideas into Action

❏ Involve managers prior to training to maximize the probability of success. This can be as simple as sending them an email about the program with a request to discuss it with their direct reports or it can be more involved, like a pre-training teleconference or training for the managers themselves.

❏ Make sure that managers are part of the plan. The most effective programs take steps to ensure that managers of trainees are a positive influence rather than a negative one.

GREATER INSIGHT D2.2

Impact of Expectations

A great deal of research has been done on how expectations shape people's attitudes and experience of reality. Many of these effects are completely subconscious; in fact, people will deny that they have been influenced in their decisions, even though you can convincingly demonstrate that they have been.

An old example that is still germane to training and development was conducted with MIT students back in the 1950s (Kelley, 1950). As students entered class, they were handed a brief biography of the guest instructor. Unbeknown to the students, there were two different versions of the sixty-three-word biography, which were identical except for two words: one described the instructor as "very warm," the other described him as "rather cold." At the end of the class, the students were all given the same questionnaire and asked to evaluate the session. As Ori and Rom

Brafman write in *Sway* (2008), "Upon seeing the results, you'd think the students were responding to two completely different instructors. Most students in the group that had received the bio describing the substitute as 'warm' loved him. . . . Although the second group sat in exactly the same class and participated in the exact same discussion, a majority of them didn't really take to the instructor" (p. 73).

If just two words can sway the experience of learning that much, it is clear that participants' preconception of the expected value of a corporate learning program will strongly influence their experience in the program as well as their post-program opinion of its value.

Areily (2010), in *Predictably Irrational,* describes numerous studies that show how people's expectations shape their experience. In a humorous example, he asked college students to taste two beers—one the standard house brew and one to which he had added a "secret ingredient." The majority preferred the beer with the "secret ingredient." However, when he used the same beers and procedure, but informed the students in advance that the "secret ingredient" was a few drops of balsamic vinegar, they overwhelmingly preferred the plain beer. Because they *expected* the beer with vinegar to taste weird, it did.

Many more cogent examples relevant to training and development can be found in Kahneman's brilliant, readable, and comprehensive *Thinking Fast and Slow* (2011).

 During Training

Obviously, what happens during the instructional period itself has a profound impact on the answer to the "Can I?" question and, hence, whether or not the training actually helps improve performance. The "during training" part of the complete experience will be discussed in more detail in D3: Deliver for Application.

After Training: A New Finish Line

What Do You Think?

1. When do you award credit or certificates for completing a training program?

   ❏ As soon as people sign up

   ❏ At the end of the class or e-learning program

   ❏ After on-the-job application

2. What message does this send?

```
notes



```

A New Paradigm Is Needed

The vast majority of training programs award credit or hand out certificates of completion at the end of the training itself. That sends the wrong message. It implies _____ and it reinforces the prevailing paradigm that all you have to do is show up and you have fulfilled your obligations.

In fact, once you focus on the business outcomes of training, you realize that "the real work begins when the class ends." The only way that training creates value for the organization is when it is put to work on the job.

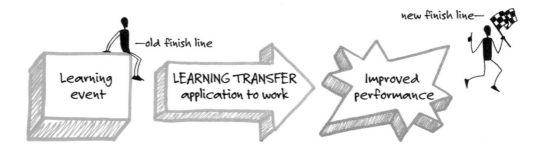

How Do You Move the Finish Line?

To reset the participants' (and their managers') expectations about what it means to complete a training program, you have to establish a criterion for completion beyond the end of the training itself (Figure D2.5). How challenging the criterion for completion is, and how rigorously it is evaluated, depend on the cost and importance of the training. The more important and expensive the training, the more rigorous the criterion for completion should be.

Examples include:

Company	New Finish Line	Notes

A Sense of Accomplishment

Setting the finish line beyond the last day of class harnesses people's intrinsic drive to succeed. Making on-the-job *performance* the requirement for earning credit or certification gives people a goal to strive for.

In *Drive: The Surprising Truth About What Motivates Us,* Daniel Pink reviewed the research on motivation and concluded that most companies greatly underestimate and underutilize the power of intrinsic rewards (such as a sense of accomplishment). This has been reinforced by Amabile and Kramer's recent study, *The Progress Principle,* which found that a sense of progress in meaningful work was associated with greater productivity, creativity, and commitment to the work.

Application to Training and Development

Amabile and Kramer conclude that: "Far too many managers are unaware of the importance of progress and therefore neither worry about or act to support it" (p. 158). Training departments are probably also "guilty as charged"; historically, we have not done enough to harness intrinsic motivation by ensuring that trainees achieve a real sense of accomplishment back on the job.

Move the Finish Line

Why This Exercise?

This exercise is an opportunity to think through—with help from your colleagues and the instructor—how you might redefine the finish line for your own program.

Instructions

1. Complete the job aid below for redefining the finish line for the program you brought to the workshop.
2. Share your ideas with colleagues and seek their input.
3. Be prepared to share your best ideas with the larger group.

New Finish Line Planner

Name of Program: E POA

What business need is the program designed to address?
(Segment 1 of Planning Wheel)

Increase *amounts* trial list of G.

What on-the-job behaviors are required to produce these results?
(Segment 2 of Planning Wheel)

Therefore, what must people do on the job to show that they have mastered (absorbed and transferred) the material?

Who can certify that this milestone has been reached in order to complete the training?

- ☒ Self-reporting sufficient
- ☐ Peer
- ☒ Manager
- ☒ Customer
- ☒ Field trainer
- ☐ Other: (please specify): _IT - IVA Utilization._

What are the specific criteria? (For example, observed it being used once, used on multiple observations, reached defined level of proficiency, produced specific results, etc.)

Field coaching Form

Reflect and Plan

Why This Exercise?

More elaborative processing results in better memory (Anderson, 2010, p. 166). Elaborative processing involves creating additional information that relates to and expands on a topic. This exercise is an opportunity for you to reflect on and elaborate the key concepts from our discussion of D2.

Instructions

1. Look back over this section and your notes.
2. Add any key ideas and relationships to the D2 (or other) branches of the 6Ds Mind Map.
3. Extend your Two Questions Mind Map by adding any associations that come to mind between D2 and the "Can I?" and "Will I?" questions.
4. Consider what actions you could take to apply D2 principles to create additional value from training. Record your ideas for action on the Road Map to Results.
5. Transfer one or two of your best ideas from your personal maps to the community maps on the wall.

Ideas into Action

❏ Think about what it really means to complete a training program.
❏ Clearly define the criteria for completion.
❏ Communicate them to both trainees and their managers.
❏ Link recognition, credit, or certificates of completion to on-the-job performance.
❏ Check the completeness of your overall design using the 6Ds Application Scorecard in the Appendix.

"If there is no commitment to all the phases of learning, you shouldn't do the program . . . just send people the bagels."
—Chris Jenkins, U.S. Bank

- Training is a process, not an event.
- Applying process improvement techniques to training increases the value that it delivers.
- What happens before and after training is as—if not more—important than the training itself.
- The learners' *complete* experience begins with the description/invitation, what they hear from prior participants, and the messages (intended and unintended) conveyed by their managers.
- Learners' *expectations* about the training affect their motivation to learn and influence their actual experience.
- Managers' actions before, during, and after training have a profound impact on its effectiveness.
- The real finish line for training is when new skills and knowledge have been transferred and applied on the job in a way that improves performance.
- A sense of making progress in meaningful work is a powerful motivator.

D3

Deliver for Application

"A great learning experience is not about the content, but about the way the content is taught."

—Julie Dirksen, *Design for How People Learn*

Only Application Produces Results

Two key themes run through this workshop:

1. Training is a means to an end; that end is ___*improved performance*___
2. Training produces improved results only when it is ___*applied*___ to the work of the individual and organization.

The third discipline—D3—is to make sure that the way in which the training is delivered facilitates its application. A complete discussion of instructional design is beyond the scope of this workshop; there are numerous books on the subject (including Julie Dirksen's very readable account quoted above) and whole graduate programs devoted to design.

Despite the substantial body of knowledge about learning and instructional design, however, many corporate learning programs are suboptimal when it comes to delivering for application. In this section, we will highlight the four most common flaws in the delivery of corporate training:

❑ Presenting too much content with too little time to practice
❑ Confusing media with method
❑ Asking the wrong questions
❑ Failing to communicate relevance and utility

"Can I?" and "Will I?" (Again)

Recall the "moment of truth" from the Introduction. Back on the job, trainees must answer two questions in the affirmative—"Can I?" and "Will I?"—for training to improve performance and pay a return to the business (Figure D3.1).

Figure D3.1. The Two Key Questions

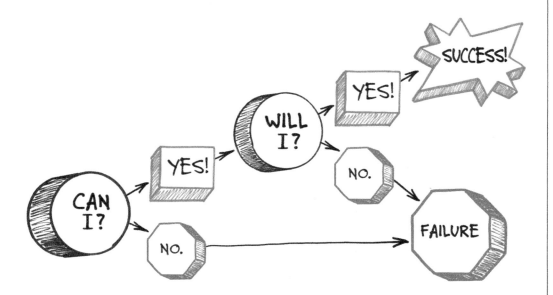

Both questions must be answered "yes" for transfer to occur, but the "Can I?" question takes precedence. Unless employees have learned *how* to do things in new and better ways, it doesn't matter how motivated they are to do so. Therefore, training and development must ensure that participants learn *how* to do what they are supposed to do. That's why D3: Deliver for Application is one of the six disciplines.

Learning, Memory, and Performance

The pathway from learning to performance can be drawn as a seven-step process (Figure D3.2). The pathway is similar for both motor skills and conceptual knowledge.

Figure D3.2. The Seven-Step Process

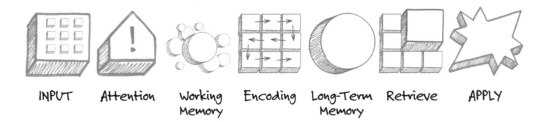

INPUT Attention Working Memory Encoding Long-Term Memory Retrieve APPLY

Step	Brief Description	Notes
INPUT	Learning starts with some kind of input.	
Attention	People must attend to the input for it to register in consciousness.	
Working Memory	Incoming information is first processed in working (short-term) memory, which has a very limited capacity.	

Encoding	Information must then be encoded into the brain's storage format and added to existing knowledge structures.	
Long-Term Memory	Knowledge and skills must be stored in long-term memory for later retrieval. This requires time and additional processing.	
Retrieve	Information must be retrieved (remembered and recalled) before it can be applied to solve a problem or accomplish a task.	
APPLY	Application requires recognizing a situation, retrieving the relevant information or skill, and adapting it to the specific situation (knowledge transfer).	

What Can Go Wrong?

Why This Exercise?

To design training that facilitates application, we need to understand the potential bottlenecks and failure points in the process. This exercise is an opportunity to identify potential issues in order to avoid them.

Instructions

1. Work with colleagues.
2. For each of the steps in the process outlined above, decide whether it is an important potential source of failure for training.
3. If so, explain why and its relevance to D3.

Step	Potential failure point?	Explain
Input	☐ Yes ☐ No	
Attention	☐ Yes ☐ No	
Working memory	☐ Yes ☐ No	
Encoding	☐ Yes ☐ No	
Long-term memory	☐ Yes ☐ No	
Retrieval	☐ Yes ☐ No	
Application	☐ Yes ☐ No	

BOTTOM LINE

There are many places at which the process of converting training to improved performance can break down. Delivering for application requires paying attention to the research on learning—especially to factors that facilitate or hinder retrieval.

Content Covered Is Not Content Learned

That training needs to teach people how to do things seems so obvious that some people have wondered why D3 was included as one of the six disciplines. The reason is summarized in Ruth Clark's famous dictum, "Content covered is not content learned" (Clark, 2010, p. 41). Just because the instructor "went over it" in class doesn't mean that people actually learned the material or that they feel confident they can use it. Too many corporate training programs emphasize "coverage" at the expense of learning.

 What Do You Think?

We can divide instruction into two main activities:

(1) content delivery and (2) practice applying the content. If the goal of training is to make sure people answer "yes" to the "Can I?" question, then:

1. What is a good ratio of content delivery to practice during training?
   a. 90% content/10% practice
   b. 67% content/33% practice
   c. 50% content/50% practice
   d. 33% content/67% practice
   e. 10% content/90% practice

2. What is the ratio of content to practice in most of your training programs today?
   a. _____ % content/_____ % practice

"The evidence, scientific as well as anecdotal, seems overwhelmingly in favor of deliberate practice as the source of great performance."

—Geoffrey Colvin, *Fortune*

The difference between what learning professionals know the ratio of content to practice should be and what it actually is in most programs is an example of what Pfeffer and Sutton (1999) called the "knowing-doing gap."

We know better. Trying to stuff "twenty pounds of content into a ten-pound sack" leads to cognitive overload. Cognitive overload reduces the amount learned and remembered. (See Greater Insight D3.1.)

GREATER INSIGHT D3.1

Cognitive Overload

Delivering too much content too quickly not only crowds out time to actively practice new skills and engage with the material, it actually *reduces* the amount that is retained and usable. Indeed, "When overload gets large enough, the learning system shuts down altogether" (Clark, Nguyen, & Sweller, 2006, p. 29). Cognitive overload overwhelms working memory and interferes with encoding and transfer to long-term memory.

Cognitive overload occurs in e-learning and multi-media programs when:

- Too many different channels are used to present information simultaneously—for example, text plus narration plus animation.
- Too many extraneous details are included in drawings, diagrams, and videos; simple line drawings are usually more educational.

Trying to stuff too much content in a program locks the instructor and participants into a forced march through the material with little time for reflection, reinforcement, or clarification. When we make time the constant and achievement the variable, some learners are inevitably left behind. Those who did not understand a foundational concept are completely lost when the instruction moves to more advanced topics that depend on a firm grasp of the basics.

Effective instruction ensures that there is enough time and active practice for participants to comprehend the material, link it to existing knowledge, and encode it in a way that facilitates its later retrieval and use. That includes returning to a key theme more than once. One of the best-studied phenomena in cognitive science is "spaced learning," the value of returning to key themes or topics at intervals. Spaced learning is both more durable and richer than when a topic is presented only once, even if the total amount of time spent is identical.

"We know from the body of research that learning occurs through the practice and feedback components. Thus, we suggest incorporating four concepts into training: information, demonstration, practice, and feedback."
—Eduardo Salas, *"The Science of Training and Development in Organizations."*

What Counts as Practice?

"Practice" in D3 means any activity that requires the learners to retrieve, select, organize, integrate, and apply new knowledge. Practice comprises much more than role play or simulations. A discussion, problem to solve, case example, relevant game, and many other activities can afford meaningful practice, provided the exercise has the following characteristics:

❏ It mirrors the way the new information and skills _need to be used on the job_. Which is rarely, if ever, just regurgitating facts.

❏ It includes _meaningful feedback_ _____.

Why Practice Matters

It is hard to over-emphasize the importance of practice. The work of Anders Ericsson, a leading researcher on human performance, has shown conclusively that the amount of deliberate practice—concentrated effort to stretch beyond one's current level of competence—is the single most important factor in developing true expertise in any area of human endeavor.

Figure D3.3. Brain Areas Engaged

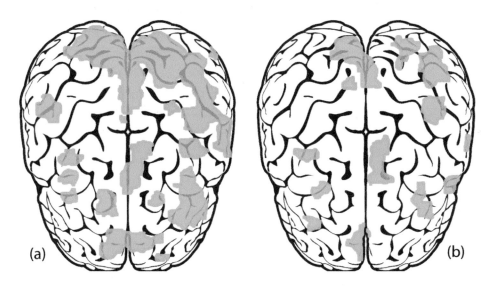

(a)   (b)

Practice improves the speed with which a task can be completed as well as reducing the amount of mental effort required. Brain imaging studies (Qin, Sohn, Anderson, et al., 2003) have shown that when people first attempt a new task or skill, many more brain areas need to be engaged (Figure D3.3a) than after it has been practiced a number of times (Figure D3.3b). With continued practice, even complex skills, like driving a car, become almost "automatic."

Figure D3.4. Time to Solution with Repeated Practice (from Anderson, 2010, p. 246, used with permission).

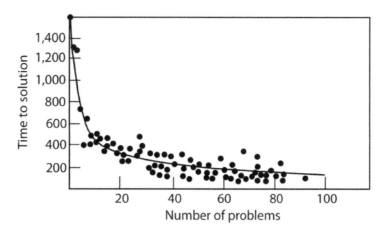

The effect of practice is a "power function." That is, improvement follows a logarithmic curve (Figure D3.4); gains are very rapid at first, but become smaller as expertise develops (Neves & Anderson, 1981). Thus, while it appears to take roughly ten thousand hours of practice to become a world champion (Ericsson, Prietula, & Cokely, 2007), even a few practice rounds in training can lead to substantial improvement.

Ideas into Action

❑ One of the most common reasons that training fails to transfer is that programs contain too much content and too little time for trainees to practice applying it.

❑ Review your program and calculate the amount of time learners sit passively hearing or seeing content versus the amount of time that they are actively engaged in applying the material.

❑ Adjust the ratio if necessary.

Share Best Practices for Providing Practice

Why This Exercise?

There are many creative and effective ways to have learners actively engage with course content. The purpose of this exercise is to tap the collective expertise of the group by sharing techniques that you have found effective for providing practice with feedback.

Instructions

1. In the chart, write one to three of the most effective techniques that you know for having participants actively practice applying what they have learned.
2. Briefly explain why for each.
3. Be prepared to share one with the group.
4. Listen to others and make notes.
5. Decide which ideas you might want to incorporate in your own programs.

notes

Best Practices I Have Used or Experienced

Brief Description	Why I Recommend It

Best Practices Presented by Others

Brief Description	Why It Sounds Potentially Useful

"Most of the time, we underestimate the amount of practice it takes to learn a new skill."

—Rosenbaum and Williams, *Learning Paths*

Application to My Own Program

I will explore adding or replacing a segment of my own program with:

_____

_____

_____

Instructional Method Versus Instructional Medium

Instructional methods are how we engage learners' minds: the way in which content and skills are introduced, conveyed, practiced, and mastered. The instructional medium, on the other hand, is just the delivery vehicle—a computer, instructor, book, smart phone, and so on.

 What Do You Think?

Which is the best tool?

❏ A hammer

❏ A saw

❏ A wrench

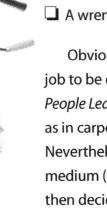

Obviously, the question can't be answered without knowing: "What is the job to be done?" The same is true for teaching methods and media. In *How People Learn,* the U.S. National Research Council concluded that: "In teaching, as in carpentry, the selection of tools depends on the task at hand" (p. 22). Nevertheless, many learning programs are designed by first selecting the medium (podcast, social media, m-learning, Articulate®, and so on) and only then deciding on the instructional method.

Where controlled trials have been done, the medium doesn't matter *as long as* _____ (Clark, 2010, p. 50). Merely repackaging an information dump to a passive learner as e-learning does not solve the core issues of information overload and inadequate practice. A lecture is a lecture is a lecture, whether delivered live, by video, webcam, or CD.

The problem with selecting the medium first is _____
_____.

When Media Matters

Why This Exercise?

The continuing wave of technological innovation has multiplied the number of potential delivery vehicles with the result that "gee-whiz" media have sometimes taken precedence over sound instructional method. This exercise is an opportunity to revisit the distinction.

Instructions

1. Collaborate with your colleagues to come up with one example each for the questions below.
2. Be prepared to share your answers with the rest of the group.

A. What is an example of an instructional need that cannot be achieved with today's e-learning or other technology?

B. What is an example of an instructional need that can be better achieved with today's e-learning or other technology than with a live (local or virtual) classroom trainer?

C. What is an example of an instructional need that can be met satisfactorily with a job aid and doesn't require any training at all?

Ideas into Action

❏ Be sure the tail isn't wagging the dog.
❏ Review a key program.
❏ Are you using technology appropriately to reduce the cost of delivery without sacrificing effectiveness?
❏ Be sure that you are not misusing costly instructor-led sessions simply to deliver content.

To satisfy D3 and deliver training that people can actually apply, decide first what has to be learned, then how best to teach it (instructional method), and *only then* the most cost-effective way to deliver it.

Asking the Wrong Questions

The third common reason that programs fail to deliver for application is that they ask the wrong questions. Given that the goal of instruction is to be sure that trainees can answer "Yes" to the "Can I?" question back on the job, it makes sense to evaluate whether, by the end of training, they have in fact learned the material and achieved an appropriate level of competence (Kirkpatrick's Level 2 or "learning" metric).

Giving a test is a great idea in theory, but usually awful in practice. Indeed, a common complaint among business managers is: "How come they can pass the test, but they can't do the job?"

What Do You Think?

Why don't most post-training assessments predict the ability to apply the training on the job?

Be Careful What You Ask For

If people know they have to pass a test at the end of the class, then that influences what they pay attention to and what they learn. If the test is mainly about regurgitating facts, then they will focus on memorizing facts to the

"People respect what you inspect."

detriment of seeking understanding or practicing skills. It's essential that the assessment reflects the performance actually required.

Sharon Shrock and Bill Coscarelli, two experts on assessment, argue that one of the single most important things you can do to improve the usefulness of post-training assessments is to make sure that the questions test more than rote recall (Shrock & Coscarelli, 2007). Rote memory questions are easy to write and grade (which is why they are so common), but they provide virtually no insight into whether learners understand or can actually apply the material.

BOTTOM LINE

If you want to know whether people can apply what they learned, then you have to test them in situations and with problems that require them to *apply,* not merely recall.

Ideas into Action

❑ Review the assessments used in your programs. Do they really measure the ability to *apply* new knowledge or skills, or merely to regurgitate minutiae?

❑ If the majority of your questions are at the recall level (and they probably will be), get some help and advice in upgrading them to test higher cognitive skills like comprehension, application, and analysis.

❑ Don't test trainees by asking them to simply play back what they learned, give them situations or problems that require them to show that they are able *to apply* what they learned.

D3 and the "Will I?" Question

Even if the training is successful in teaching employees new and better ways to do their jobs (they can answer "Yes" to the "Can I?" question), that still doesn't guarantee that they will transfer and apply what they learned. They also have to answer "Yes" to the "Will I?" question. "Will I?" is a question of motivation: Are learners sufficiently motivated that they will make the effort to apply new learning? (Figure D3.5).

Figure D3.5. Will I?

A useful model for thinking about the motivation to apply new skills at work is Vroom's Expectancy Model (Figure D3.6), which says that effort is proportional to motivation and that motivation is driven by:

❑ _____

❑ _____

❑ _____

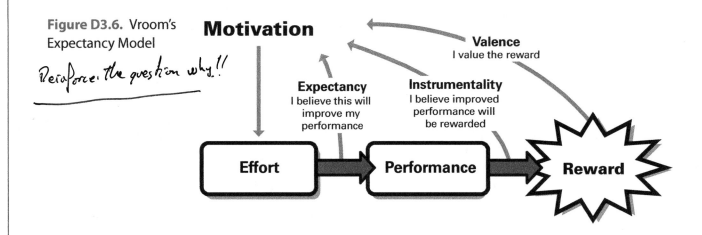

Figure D3.6. Vroom's Expectancy Model

Reinforce the question why!!

Motivation

Expectancy
I believe this will improve my performance

Instrumentality
I believe improved performance will be rewarded

Valence
I value the reward

Effort → Performance → Reward

"The need to know affects motivation to learn, learning outcomes, and post-training motivation to use learning."

—Knowles, Holton, and Swanson, *The Adult Learner*

We need to "make the sale" that the training is relevant and useful before people will learn it and, having learned it, apply it.

Show Me the Relevance

One of the key principles of adult learning is that adults want to know _____*Why*_____ they are being asked to learn something before they will do so willingly.

It is not surprising, therefore, that a perceived lack of relevance is one of the major barriers to training effectiveness. Two questions are on every trainee's mind:

❏ "Why am I here?" and
❏ "What's in it for me?" (WIIFM)

An important aspect of Delivering for Application it to make sure that those questions are addressed. You may have noticed that each exercise in this workshop begins with the question "Why this exercise?" for just that reason. (See Greater Insight D3.2: Introducing Exercises.)

GREATER INSIGHT D3.2

Introducing Exercises

Adult learners want to understand the relevance of the training program to their jobs. They also want to know why they are being asked to do each exercise, especially the ones (like role play) that are more work and "less fun." Although the purpose of each exercise and topic is usually clear to instructional designers, it is often lost on the participants.

One reason is that exercises are typically introduced using an "administrative" approach—explaining the "how" (how much time, size of groups) without first explaining the "why" (benefits, WIIFM).

Margolis and Bell (1986) proposed that you should always introduce exercises in a four-step process:

1. Make the rationale clear.
2. Explain the task.
3. Define "how."
4. Clarify what is to be reported.

"This sequence follows the logic of learning and the logic of motivation. . . . The introduction/rationale is a statement that answers a fundamental question for the learner: 'Why should I enter into this task or experience?'" (p. 70).

Starting each exercise by explaining the rationale acknowledges a fundamental requirement of adult learning: adults want to know "why?"

Linking Up the Value Chain

One way to ensure the relevance of training is to draw a value chain. Michael Porter (1985) originated the concept of a value chain to describe the sequence of value-adding activities by which a company creates competitive advantage. Like Brinkerhoff and Gill's (1994) "impact map," a value chain for learning describes the value-adding activities of training by illustrating the links between learning and business results.

The value chain for training has three main links (Figure D3.7).

Figure D3.7. The Value Chain for Learning

The first two links come directly from the Planning Wheel (Figure D3.8), in accordance with Stephen Covey's famous dictum to "begin with the end in mind."

The third link—the specific training content and activities—are developed by applying instructional design expertise to answer the question: "What is the best way to teach someone to ensure that they can do what is required (Link 2) to achieve the results we need (Link 1)?"

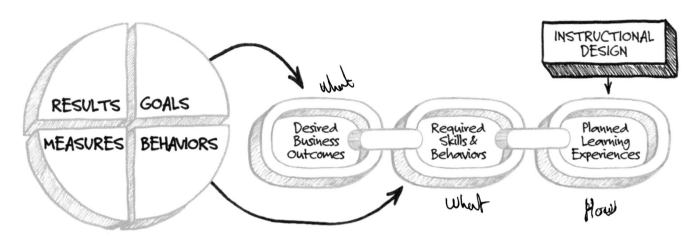

Figure D3.8. Connecting D1 to D3

Your Turn

Apply the Value Chain

Why This Exercise?

This is an opportunity to experiment with using a job aid—the value chain—by applying it to your own program. The value chain can be used in one of two ways:

❏ During program design to help decide how best to teach so that learners are able to do what they need to be able to do

❏ For quality control of a completed design

In this instance, we will be using it for the latter application, to test the linkage between the instructional (D3) plan and the D1 Outcomes being pursued.

Instructions

1. Select two or three topics or exercises from the program you brought to work on.
2. List them in the third column of the table on page 103.
3. Now review your D1 Planning Wheel.
4. Put the overall business purpose in the first column and the required behaviors in the middle column.
5. Try to draw links between the learning components, the required behaviors, and the desired results.
6. Answer the following questions about each topic or exercise you have mapped:
    a. Does it have a clear relationship to one or more of the required behaviors/skills?
       ❏ If no, then either the D1 analysis was incomplete or this item has no direct relevance to the aim of the course and should be eliminated.
    b. If there is a strong link, will it be obvious to the participants?
       ❏ If not, how could the relevance be made more explicit?
    c. Assuming the element is relevant, does the instructional method match the required output? (Is there enough practice, for example?)
7. Be prepared to share some examples with the group.

Table D3.3. Value Chain

Desired Business Outcomes	Required Skills and Behaviors	Planned Learning Experiences

But Will It Help Me?

Failure to effectively communicate training's relevance and utility is a fourth common source of learning scrap. Recall that in Vroom's motivation model (Figure D3.6), a key factor that drives motivation and effort is the strength of the *belief* that making the effort will lead to improved performance. So we need to not only teach relevant skills and approaches, but we also need to *persuade* learners that using them will pay off for them personally.

What Do You Think?

What can you do in the invitation, course description, and during instruction to help convince people that if they make the effort to master and use the new material, it will pay off for them in improved performance?

My ideas:

Good ideas from others:

It's Clear to You; Is It Clear to Them?

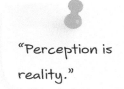

"Perception is reality."

Even if you try to make the course practical and useful, you cannot always be sure that the message will get through. For that reason, you need to monitor the *perceived* relevance and utility on end-of-course evaluations (see Ideas into Action below).

What Do You Think?

Numerous studies have shown that end-of-course reactions (Kirkpatrick's Level 1) don't correlate with how much people learned or whether they will use it. Nevertheless, we recommend asking people to rate the *perceived* usefulness and relevance at the end of training.

Why?

Ideas into Action

To assess the *perceived* relevance and utility of the training, ask participants to rate the following statements immediately following instruction (Level 1 evaluation):

1. What I learned is directly relevant to my job.
   ○ Strongly disagree   ○ Disagree   ○ Agree   ○ Strongly agree

2. Using what I learned will improve my performance.
   ○ Strongly disagree   ○ Disagree   ○ Agree   ○ Strongly agree

3. I feel I am well prepared to use what I learned.
   ○ Strongly disagree   ○ Disagree   ○ Agree   ○ Strongly agree

4. I am motivated to put my learning to work.
   ○ Strongly disagree   ○ Disagree   ○ Agree   ○ Strongly agree

While positive immediate post-course reactions do not necessarily predict application, low perceived relevance scores need to be investigated and addressed. They do not necessarily mean that the course was not relevant or useful, but they suggest that learners won't make much of an effort to apply the training. Review programs that score low on relevance or utility to understand the root cause. Table D3.2 lists some of the most common causes of low relevance/utility ratings.

What's possible if you do this.

Do they proceed on utilization and relevance.

Table D3.2. Common Causes of Low Utility/Relevance Ratings

Cause	Explanation
Wrong audience	The training really was not relevant to these learners' job responsibilities; they should not have been there in the first place.
Wrong timing	The training was not relevant to the learners' current job responsibilities and the design did not adequately create a "need to know" regarding future responsibilities.
Wrong examples	The audience was unable to relate to the examples used in the training and the instructors were not able to build credible bridges.
No sale	There was not enough evidence that using the techniques taught would truly benefit the employees, or the evidence was not presented in a convincing manner.
Too much material or too theoretical	The message was lost in an onslaught of too much material or too much theory without enough practical application.
Wrong instructional methods	The instructional methods did not allow opportunities for learners to experience the relevance and utility for themselves.
Bad attitude	Learners arrived at the training already convinced that it was not relevant or useful as a result of what they heard from their managers, peers, or former attendees. This expectation became a self-fulfilling prophecy.

D3
DELIVER
FOR APPLICATION

Your Turn

Reflect and Plan

Why This Exercise?

Cognitive research has shown that elaborating on an idea or concept increases the ability to remember and later retrieve it. One of the best ways to do that is "elaborative rehearsal" in which you explain or re-tell the concept to someone else. This exercise gives you the opportunity to share something that we have discussed with a colleague in order to help form connections that are relevant and useful to you.

Instructions

1. Look back over this section and your notes.
2. Turn to the person next to you and explain what, in particular, stood out for you from the discussion as well as any connections you made to other topics from this course or others.
3. Change roles.
4. Add some key ideas as branches, twigs, and connections to your mind maps.
5. Finally, consider how you can apply D3. Record your ideas for putting learning into action on the Road Map to Results.
6. Transfer one or two of your best ideas from your personal maps to sticky notes and post them on the community maps.

SUMMING UP

- Since the ultimate goal of training is to improve on-the-job performance, corporate programs need to be designed and delivered with special emphasis on application.

- How training is delivered—in particular the instructional methods used—affect the answers to both the "Can I?" and "Will I?" questions.

- Converting learning into performance is a multi-step process; breakdowns can occur at any step from attention to retrieval.

- The four most common pitfalls to delivering for application are
  - Presenting too much content with too little time to practice
  - Allowing instructional media to trump instructional method
  - Testing recall rather than application
  - Failing to effectively communicate training's relevance and utility

- Practice increases the speed with which a task can be performed and reduces the mental effort required to do so.

- Performance improvement is fastest at the beginning; even a few practice sessions can produce significant improvement in new skills.

- The instructional method should be selected first, then the medium by which to convey it.

- Not all media can support all methods.

- If participants are not convinced that the training is relevant and useful to them, they won't make an effort to transfer and apply it.

- Therefore, it is important to monitor and manage the *perceived* relevance and utility of training programs.

D4 **Drive Learning Transfer**

"To change behavior and get the results you want, you need structure, support, and accountability."

—Ken Blanchard, *Know Can Do!*

Hope Is Not a Strategy

Learning transfer is essential to convert training into business results (Figure D4.1).

Although this concept is well known, most instructional designs fail to include the "structure, support, and accountability" necessary to ensure that learning is transferred, behaviors change, and performance improves (Figure D4.2).

For training and development to achieve its full potential, we need to do more than hope that a miracle will convert training into business results.

In naming D4, we chose the verb "drive" intentionally. Experience has proven that hoping for transfer is not a successful strategy. Organizations have to drive learning transfer, just as athletes have to drive to the finish line and business managers have to drive for profits and revenue. Given the magnitude of the investment in learning and its importance to business success, companies should hold employees accountable for applying their training to their work.

Figure D4.1. Learning Transfer

Figure D4.2. Why Learning Transfer Often Fails

© Sidney Harris/The New Yorker Collection/ www.cartoonbank.com. Used with permission.

"I think you should be more explicit here in step two."

D4
DRIVE
LEARNING TRANSFER

A Process Approach

↓ 1 one of 300,000
↑

Process improvement methodologies (Total Quality Management, Six Sigma, Kaizen, and the like) have enabled companies to consistently produce higher-quality goods at lower cost. Many manufacturing companies now routinely achieve Six Sigma quality: less than one defect per _____ units.

The original goal of process improvement was to reduce the amount of manufacturing scrap—parts or products that did not meet the customers' requirements and, as a result, had to be discarded or remanufactured.

 What Do You Think?

Why were manufacturers so driven to reduce scrap? Confer with your colleagues and come up with the costs—both tangible and intangible—of manufacturing scrap:

Tangible Costs of Manufacturing Scrap	Intangible Costs of Manufacturing Scrap
time	Customer engagement.

Process improvement can be applied to any business process. It has increased the quality and reduced the costs of customer service, transaction processing, inventory management, problem resolution, and many others, including training. (See Greater Insight D4.1: Process Improvement.)

D4
DRIVE
LEARNINGTRANSFER

GREATER INSIGHT D4.1

Process Improvement

Process improvement is the core tenet of a number of related concepts including Total Quality Management, Process Reengineering, Six Sigma, Kaizen, Zero Defects, Lean, and many others.

Three Americans: Shewhart, Deming, and Juran, are generally credited with developing the methodology and of applying statistical process control to quality improvement. It was the Japanese, however, who first embraced the concepts as a key part of their strategy to rebuild their economy after World War II. Over time, these quality initiatives began to pay off: so much so that in the 1980s, Ford Motor Company finally asked Deming to help them implement a quality initiative because they realized how far they had fallen behind their Japanese competitors.

Process improvement methodology can be applied to any business process, including the delivery of services, with similar gains in effectiveness and efficiency. For example, by applying Lean Six Sigma processes, the City of Fort Wayne, Indiana:

- Cut the time required to complete a fire code re-inspection by an average of thirty-four days
- Increased the number of inspections that could be completed by 23 percent with no increase in staff
- Increased the percent of potholes that were repaired in twenty-four hours from 77 to 98 percent
- Reduced the number of Parks Department complaints by 33 percent (George, 2003)

All process improvement efforts are based on three fundamental questions:

- What are we trying to accomplish?
- What changes can we make that will result in an improvement?
- How will we know that the change is an improvement? (Langley, Moen, Nolan, Nolan, Norman, & Provost, 2009, p. 24)

Continuous process improvement consists of asking these questions over and over, making adjustments to the system, measuring the results, and using the knowledge gained to make further refinements (Plan-Do-Check-Act).

Learning Scrap

In the Introduction, we introduced the term "learning scrap" to refer to training that employees attend but never apply. It is the training and development equivalent of manufacturing scrap.

 What Do You Think?

What are the costs—both tangible and intangible—of learning scrap? Confer briefly with your colleagues to complete the table below:

Tangible Costs of Learning Scrap	Intangible Costs of Learning Scrap

BOTTOM LINE

Learning scrap, like manufacturing scrap, carries a high cost in terms of wasted time, labor, materials, and opportunity cost. Learning scrap is also the major cause of customer dissatisfaction with training and development. Therefore, reducing learning scrap needs to be a high priority for training professionals.

Business Case for Learning Transfer

Initially, companies resisted quality improvement programs. They saw them as simply adding cost. Only when their competitors (most notably Japanese car companies in the 1970s) began winning market share with higher-quality and lower-cost products did management appreciate the business rationale for investing in quality improvement.

Can we make a similar case for investing to improve learning transfer?

Business Case for Learning Transfer

Why This Exercise?

Managers have to make decisions based on what is best for the business. Training and development needs to be able to make a *business case* for investing more time and effort to drive learning transfer. The goal of this exercise is to give you insights that will help you do so.

Instructions

Situation 1: The results of two programs (–D4 and +D4) are shown in the table below. The nature of the training made it possible to determine who did and did not transfer what they learned and to calculate the financial value of doing so.

In both programs, the training itself was identical. The only difference is that +D4 also included active support for learning transfer as part of the design.

The cost of adding learning transfer support to +D4 was $200 per participant—a 20 percent increase in the cost of the program.

1. Confer with your colleagues.
2. Decide which program (–D4 or +D4) below makes better *business sense* (in terms of the return on investment) and why.
3. Be prepared to share your conclusion and rationale.

	Program –D4	Program +D4
Number of participants	100	100
Cost per participant	$1,000	$1,200
Transfer rate (percent who truly applied the training)	20 percent	30 percent
Return per person who applied training	$6,000	$6,000
ROI* for program		

*Return on Investment (ROI) = (return – cost) / cost

Situation 2: In the above example, training and development persuaded management to increase the budget for the program to include the cost of transfer based on the projected return. But suppose that, despite the improved return, there simply is no more money?

Would it be a better business proposition to reduce the number of trainees in order to support transfer, or stay with the original plan?

The next table is identical to the one above, except that the number of trainees in program +D4 has been reduced from 100 to 87 to stay within the program budget of $100,000.

1. Confer with your colleagues.
2. Decide which of the programs below makes better *business sense* (in terms of return on investment) and why.
3. Be prepared to share your recommendation and rationale with the larger group.

	Program –D4	Program +D4 (with fewer participants)
Number of participants	100	87
Cost per participant	$1,000	$1,200
Transfer rate (percent who truly applied the training)	20 percent	30 percent
Return per person who applied training	$6,000	$6,000
ROI for program		

notes

← ———————— % Unrealized ————————| % Realized!

Figure D4.3. Unrealized Value vs. Realized Value of Typical Training Programs

In the above examples, the transfer rate increased from the typical 20 percent to only 30 percent. Even so, the additional value to the organization was substantial. Imagine the improvement that would result if you rigorously applied the 6Ds and increased the transfer rate to 40, 60, or 80 percent.

Why are the results so dramatic? Because at the low transfer rates typical of most training programs today _____

_____

(Figure D4.3).

BOTTOM LINE

Learning scrap is a terrible waste of time, talent, and resources on training that is never used. It makes economic sense to invest in increasing learning transfer.

Real-World Results

The above examples are hypothetical and simplified (although not atypical). Does investing in learning transfer produce these kinds of results in the real world of business? The evidence is that is does.

For example, an independent, controlled study conducted by Pfizer reported a more than 40 percent increase in the dollarized benefits of a leadership development program after an online learning transfer support system was added (Figure D4.4).

Of course, not all programs can (or should) be analyzed in financial terms (as we will discuss in D6: Document Results). The amount of learning transfer can still be assessed by other means—such as observations, self-reports,

Figure D4.4. Added Value with Transfer Support

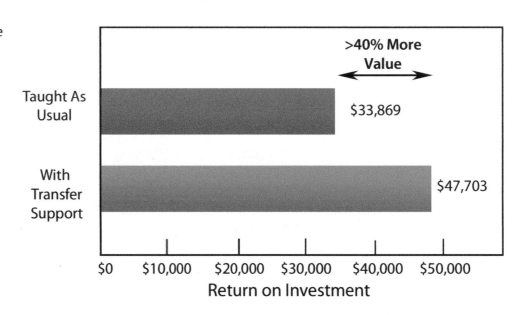

achievement stories, customer surveys, and so forth. Providing support and accountability for transfer also produces significant improvement when these measures are used.

Process Improvement

Turning training into business results is a process that can be enhanced by the application of process improvement methods. While a full discussion of process improvement is beyond the scope of this workshop, three techniques are especially relevant to reducing learning scrap:

1. Identify root causes.
2. Harvest low-hanging fruit.
3. Plan-Do-Check-Act (PDCA).

"Based on results from a wide variety of organizations, the research showed learning transfer can be increased by as much as 180 percent, with only modest cost increases."

—Leimbach and Emde, *Chief Learning Officer*

Root Causes

Identifying root causes means _____ _____ and getting to the real heart of the issue. For example, you might find that employees aren't transferring their learning from a particular program because they are not sufficiently motivated to make the effort (they answer "No" to the "Will I?" question). You need to conduct a root-cause analysis to understand *why* they are not motivated and identify the specific actions required to correct the problem.

Root Causes

Why This Exercise?

To improve a process, you need to identify the most important root causes of failure. This exercise is an opportunity to prioritize the most common reasons that training fails to improve performance.

Instructions

We have listed four key contributors to learning scrap below:

1. Working with your colleagues, assign the relative percentage contribution of each. In other words, what percent of training failures is due to each factor?
2. Be prepared to report out.

Factor	Percent of Training Failures
Training was not the right solution to the performance issue	10
Wrong audience or wrong timing	10
The training itself was ineffective	20
Inadequate structure, support, and accountability after training	60
Total	100%

Low-Hanging Fruit

In process improvement terms, "low-hanging fruits" are issues that are _relatively easy to fix big pay off_. The analogy is to low-hanging apples that can be picked without a ladder or much effort. At the beginning of process improvement, there are always a number of such low-hanging fruits. These should be identified and acted upon first.

PDCA

A fundamental tool of process improvement is the PDCA Cycle (also called the PDSA or Deming Cycle, shown in Figure D4.5). The concept is simple. Once you have identified an opportunity for improvement, **P**lan a change to the process, **D**o it, **C**heck (or **S**tudy) the results, and **A**ct (or **A**djust) based on your findings.

Having identified the key contributors to training failures, we need to develop plans (P) to reduce them, implement the plans (D), check the results (C) and act (A) on the outcomes. We will return to the PDCA Cycle in our discussion of evaluation in D6.

Figure D4.5. The PDCA Cycle

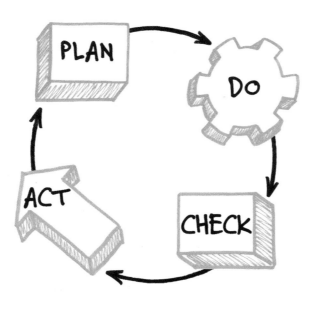

"Creating a high-transfer climate should swiftly move to the forefront of any training initiative or strategy."

—American Express

Transfer Climate

While all six Ds impact learning transfer, the post-instruction transfer climate is especially important. Indeed, a study at American Express concluded that: "The true impact of a training program will best be predicted by the work climate each participant returns to after the event . . . these climate factors can quite literally make or break your training investments" (American Express, 2007).

But what is the transfer climate? Rouiller and Goldstein defined the learning transfer climate as: _____
_____ .

What Do You Think?

Based on your own experiences and those of your colleagues, what do you think are the key components of the transfer climate? Put an asterisk next to the two or three that you think have the greatest impact:

Key elements of the transfer climate include:

BOTTOM LINE

The transfer climate is critical because it determines the answer to the "Will I?" question. Even if the training enabled trainees to answer the "Can I?" question in the affirmative, it still creates no value to the enterprise unless they also answer "Yes" to the "Will I?" question. So, while training and development does not *control* the elements of the transfer climate, our effectiveness depends on our ability to positively influence them.

WILL I?

Am I motivated to make the effort?

DO I THINK IT WILL HELP ME?

Will anybody notice if I do?
What do my peers and my boss think?

A Transfer Climate Model

Holton and his colleagues at Louisiana State University (Holton, Bates, & Ruona, 2000) developed a model for thinking about and assessing the transfer climate, which they called the Learning Transfer Systems Inventory (LTSI). The complete inventory comprises fifty-one questions grouped into sixteen factors, under three major headings (Figure D4.6):

❏ Ability to use
❏ Motivation to use
❏ Environmental catalysts or impediments

Figure D4.6. Major Elements of the Transfer Climate

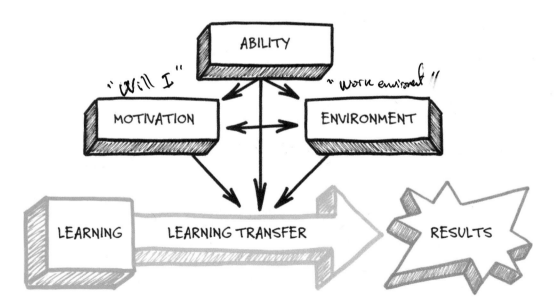

Rate Your Transfer Climate

Why This Exercise?

The success of training—in terms of delivering business results—is determined as much by the transfer climate as by the quality of the training itself. This exercise is an opportunity to practice using a job aid to assess the transfer climate for your program and to think about specific actions you can take to positively influence that climate.

Instructions

1. Rate the transfer climate for your program using the job aid below.
2. Identify the two lowest-scoring factors.
3. Compare answers with your colleagues.
4. Use the Transfer Climate Change Planner in the Appendix to identify potential actions to improve the weakest areas of your climate.

Key impediment to transfer

Learning Transfer Climate Scorecard

Rate each of the climatic factors below on the scale shown. Use the descriptors below each item to help you.

Climatic Factor	0. Very Weak	1. Weak	2. Fairly Strong	3. Very Strong	? Don't Know
Learner Readiness Learners understand what the training is about and how it relates to their development and job performance. Learners have the necessary background knowledge and skills to benefit from the training.				✗	
Opportunity to Use Employees have opportunities to apply their new knowledge and skills on the job soon after training. Employees have the resources (information, equipment, materials, and supplies) necessary to use the training.			✗		
Personal Capacity Employees have the time and energy to try new methods; their workloads are not too overwhelming. Employees are able to cope with the amount and pace of change in the organization.			✗		

Climatic Factor	0	1	2	3	?
Perceived Relevance and Utility Employees feel that the skills and knowledge taught are relevant and useful to their work. The instructional methods, aids, materials, and equipment used in training are similar to those used on the job.				✗	
Motivation Employees are motivated to use what they learned because they: • Are convinced it will help them perform better • Expect better performance to be rewarded in a way that they value				✗	
Organizational Culture Performance expectations are clear. Individuals are recognized for good performance. People feel good about performing well.			✗		
Managerial Alignment Managers speak positively about the techniques taught. Managers model the same approaches, behaviors, and skills as those taught in training. Managers set clear expectations for the application of training.			✗		

Climatic Factor	0	1	2	3	?
Managerial Encouragement Managers encourage the use of new skills. Managers recognize individuals who make the effort to apply their learning.			X		
Managerial Feedback and Coaching Employees receive constructive input and assistance from their managers when they try to apply what they learned. Managers assist individuals when they encounter problems as they try to apply new learning.				X	
Peer Group Impact The employees' co-workers support the use of new techniques; they don't try to force conformity to current practice. Peers help each other identify opportunities and implement new methods.				X	
Personal Experience Employees experience positive benefits from using what they have learned, such as increased productivity, recognition, additional opportunities, or the like. Employees experience negative consequences for *not using* what they learned, such as criticism or reprimands. But there are *no negative consequences* when they try to apply their learning to their work.				X	

Adapted from the Learning Transfer Systems Inventory, Audit Format, Holton, 2003.

The two lowest-scoring items in the transfer climate for my program are

1. _Opportunity to use_
2. _Personal capacity_

Actions I could take to improve these areas include:

1. _Align Mng feedback & coaching_
2. _Align Peer & Mans encorage._

If you scored one or more items as "Don't Know," then you need to investigate these aspects of the transfer climate to find out whether they are enhancing or detracting from your training efforts.

Ideas into Action

❏ Incorporate the transfer climate scorecard into planning for critical programs.

❏ Engage business leaders in scoring it and discussing the results.

❏ Explain the profound impact of the transfer climate and why it is essential to manage it.

Low-Hanging Fruit: Reminders

One relatively easy-to-implement process that helps drive learning transfer is simply to remind people about the training and their need to apply it.

What Do You Think?

McDonald's is one of the best-known brand names on the planet. Yet they continue to spend millions of dollars on advertising. If everybody already knows that McDonald's sells fast food, why do they continue to advertise? Put your heads together with your colleagues and list the reasons you think McDonald's continues to advertise:

McDonalds continues to advertise because . . .

Application to Training and Development

What does McDonald's have to do with training and development? They—and all other successful brands—have learned that you have to remind people often if you want your message to stay top-of-mind and lead to action.

What lesson can we learn? If we want to keep the application of new skills and knowledge top-of-mind, then _We need to remind people periodically training._ Otherwise, we'll lose share of mind and day-to-day tasks will overwhelm good intentions to apply learning.

Reminders can take many forms (think how many different ways advertisers use to present their message):

- ❏ Emails or other communications
- ❏ Tips on application (podcasts, vodcasts, and so on)
- ❏ New content, information, or ways to use the training
- ❏ Posters, mugs, screensavers, etc.
- ❏ Questions and quizzes

The key thing is to gain people's attention and cause them to reactivate the memory pathways to what they learned. There is solid learning theory behind this: Every time you retrieve information, you *strenghten the neural conextion to it*, which makes it easier to recall and use in the future.

To provide reminders to dozens or hundreds of users, you will need to automate the process. Fortunately, there is now commercial learning transfer support software to help you, social media, and a variety of "push" technologies.

But What About Email Overload? *Qstream came out of Harvard med school*

Everyone complains about the amount of email they receive. Nevertheless,

in controlled trials, people who received emails reminding them about their goal of changing to healthier habits were much more successful than those who did not receive reminders. Likewise, studies at the Harvard Medical School have shown that medical students who received a series of questions by email at weekly intervals showed much greater learning retention later than those who simply attended class (Kerfoot & Brotschi, 2009).

Ideas into Action

❏ Investigate commercially available learning transfer support systems. Experiment and see what works in your culture/program.

❏ Stimulate recall and reflection by posing questions or providing tips and supplemental material periodically during the learning transfer period.

Managers and the "Will I?" Question

What Do You Think?

Who is the single most important person in your organization when it comes to ensuring learning transfer?

In my organization, it is: _The immediate direct manager/leader_

According to Kouzes and Posner's *The Leadership Challenge*:

> "If you're a manager in an organization, to your direct reports you are the most important leader in your organization. You are more likely than any other leader to influence their desire to stay or leave, the trajectory of their careers, their ethical behavior, their ability to perform at their best, their drive to wow customers, their satisfaction with their jobs, and their motivation to share the organization's vision and values." (2007, p. 338)

They could have easily added "and their willingness to make the effort to apply training."

As the following examples illustrate, managers have a profound impact on learning transfer.

	Study	Conclusions
1		
2		

A learner's direct supervisor creates an environment that is either conducive or corrosive to the application of learning, which is why American Express concluded that: "an immediate leader has the potential to either ___Make or Break___ any training effort."

But doesn't the learner have some responsibility? Of course. The great management guru Peter Drucker pointed out that "all development is self-development." But the transfer climate—and the manager's reactions, in particular—encourage or discourage self-development.

So, What's the Problem?

Given that managers can significantly accelerate learning transfer, and given that better-performing employees help the manager get ahead, why don't managers coach more?

Rank the Impediments

Why This Exercise?

Increasing the amount of managerial support will increase learning transfer and boost results. This exercise is an opportunity to review and rank the root causes of manager disengagement as a first step to designing solutions.

> "Trainees must be encouraged and supported to commit, engage, and persist at transfer."
>
> —Harold Stolovitch, *Training Ain't Performance*

Instructions

1. Review the list below of the common reasons that managers don't coach.
2. Rank order them from 1 (most important in your organization) to 9, least important.
3. Compare your rankings with those of your colleagues.

Reason	Your Ranking
I don't have the time; this is not a priority for me.	
I am not held accountable or rewarded for coaching.	
I don't really know what I am supposed to do.	
I don't know what the program was about; I have never attended it.	
I don't agree with what they are teaching over there.	
I didn't have any input into the program or its contents.	
I am just not comfortable coaching people.	
I don't know what my direct reports are supposed to do with what they learned.	
Other: _____	

The top two impediments to greater managerial support post-training for my program are

1. _____

2. _____

notes

What Is Working?

Every training organization struggles to engage line managers. Some, however, have found creative and effective ways to do so (See Greater Insight D4.2: Engaging Managers). If you are doing something that is having a positive effect, please share it with your colleagues so that we all get smarter and more effective.

Good Ideas I Heard from Others

D4
DRIVE
LEARNING TRANSFER

GREATER INSIGHT D4.2

Engaging Managers

Given the influence of managers on the learning transfer process, it is virtually impossible to achieve significant performance improvement after training without managerial support. Managers are an integral and crucial part of the total system for helping employees apply learning and convert it into business results.

That's why Agilent CEO Bill Sullivan wanted to start cascading Agilent's new, business-focused, applied-learning experience down from the top. He told his chief learning officer Teresa Roche: "Let's make sure the soil is fertile so that when people come out of their experience, they have a manager and a set of colleagues who are getting what they are talking about and we can have better transfer and application."

"Managerial coaching has a significant positive influence. . ."

—Watkins and Leigh, *Handbook of Improving Performance in the Workplace*

Geoff Rip, president of ChangeLever International, a learning transfer consulting firm, feels so strongly about the benefits of managerial support that he holds a special course for managers in advance of training their subordinates. The program for managers focuses on how they can and should use their influence to ensure transfer and extend learning, thereby maximizing the benefits to their department.

Lisa Bell, manager of the North American Learning Center for Holcim, held day-long "impact booster" sessions for managers of participants in the company's Building Leader Performance Program. She is convinced that they were a key factor in the program's success. Bell felt so strongly about the value of these sessions that she resisted pressure to shorten them. "Initially, one of our biggest concerns was that managers would never give up their precious time to participate in the 'extra' steps we asked of them. And now, lo and behold, they themselves have asked for more."

When it is impossible or impractical to provide specific training for managers, provide them with a practical guide with advice on how to maximize the benefits of their reports' education, as Diane Hinton does at Plastipak. Plastipak's High Impact Learning Job Aid for Supervisors provides managers with step-by-step guidance for preparing the learners before training and following up effectively afterward.

Make the guide concise, practical, and action-oriented. Provide easy-to-use forms, step-by-step processes, and examples. Send out copies to managers in advance of training and make it easily accessible in both print and online versions.

Adapted from Wick, Pollock, and Jefferson, 2010, *The Six Disciplines of Breakthrough Learning.* References in the original.

Turn Learning into Action

Why This Exercise?

Learning adds value only when it is converted to action. This is an opportunity to think about and plan specific steps to improve managerial support for training transfer.

Instructions

1. Refer to the notes you just made and to the "Getting Managers More Engaged" job aid below.
2. Select two or three specific actions you can take to improve managerial reinforcement of your program.
3. Complete the chart below and transfer your ideas for action to your Road Map to Results.

Getting Managers More Engaged	
Current issue or impediment:	**What I will do to address it:**

Learning Transfer After This Workshop

We need to "practice what we preach." So this workshop will not end after D6. Instead, you'll be asked to set a personal goal to accomplish by applying insights or tools from the workshop.

We will remind you every couple of weeks for the next two months about your goal. You'll be asked to stop and reflect on your progress and what you need to do next to achieve your goal. We'll be available as coaches throughout the process to assist you.

The "finish line" for this workshop is when you can report how you have applied the 6Ds to create additional value for your organization.

Reflect and Learn Plan

Why This Exercise?

This exercise gives you the opportunity to stop and reflect on what we have discussed and to form connections that are the most meaningful to you in your work. Doing so will help you later recall and use key concepts.

Instructions

1. Look back over this section and your notes.
2. Answer one or more of the following questions:
    a. I hadn't realized before that . . .
    b. I hadn't considered before that . . .
    c. I hadn't thought before that . . .
    d. I hadn't noticed before that . . .
3. Tell one of the ideas to the person next to you.
4. Transfer your best ideas to your personal maps and to the community maps on the wall.

SUMMING UP

- Lack of transfer is the main reason that training often fails to improve performance.

- To change behavior and obtain results, you need structure, support, and accountability.

- You cannot simply hope that participants will transfer what they learned; D4 needs to be part of the overall instructional design.

- Transforming training into business results is a process; it can and should be continuously improved by applying process-improvement tools and methods.

- The post-training "transfer climate" determines the answer to the "Will I?" question and, therefore, whether learning is applied or becomes scrap.

- The transfer climate includes all those environmental clues that indicate whether or not using the training is perceived as important.

- The most important single factor in the transfer climate is the trainees' manager; he or she can make or break the success of any training initiative.

D5 Deploy
Performance
Support

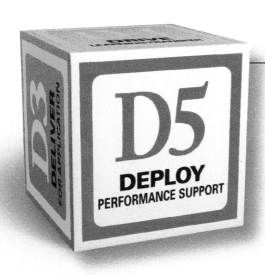

"Help, I need somebody!

Help, not just anybody."

—The Beatles

Support Is Part of the Complete Experience

Nowadays, most consumer products—from simple devices like refrigerators to complex ones like cars or computers—come with substantial customer support. In addition to owner's manuals, there are now apps, online help, toll-free support lines, users' groups, live chat, and more.

What Do You Think?

Why do companies invest so much time and so much effort providing support for products you have already purchased? What benefit do they expect the support to produce?

Confer with your colleagues and list your ideas below.

> Companies expect to get a return on their investment in support through . . .

Application to Training and Development

Consumer product companies have figured out that the ability to use a product well—which includes the availability of help when the consumer has a question or problem—is part of the "whole product experience." And the whole product experience determines whether people will buy the same brand again, as well as what they tell others.

What's the application to training and development? Providing performance support after training affects the answer to the "Can I?" question (Figure D5.1). If trainees know they will be able to obtain assistance if they run into difficulties, they are more willing to try to apply new learning to their work.

The right kind of performance support also ensures that employees follow procedures correctly. That's important in many jobs in which omitting or mis-performing a step can lead to serious safety, legal, or business consequences.

Figure D5.1. A Fundamental Question

The better that people are able to apply their training, the more satisfied both they and their managers will be. The more satisfied they are, the more willing they will be to support training in the future.

BOTTOM LINE
Performance support increases learning transfer and the business value of training; it should be a required part of every training design.

What Is Performance Support?

Performance support is anything that helps employees *do things right*. It can take many forms, from simple paper-based job aids to sophisticated online databases or troubleshooting algorithms.

Best Examples

Why This Exercise?

This is an opportunity to expand your thinking about performance support with specific and successful examples from the collective wisdom and experience of the group.

Ideas into Action

❏ Review your training design process.

❏ Does it require consideration of post-training support?

❏ If not, make it part of the overall design process.

Instructions

1. Think about the most useful performance support you have ever experienced (used yourself or created). Include examples from outside corporate training.

2. Briefly describe the support below.

3. Share with your colleagues.

Best Performance Support Ever

Briefly describe the support (what it was and how it was delivered):

What did it help you accomplish?

What made it so great? (Why did you choose this particular example?)

Characteristics of Great Performance Support

There are many different ways to deliver performance support—from simply pasting instructions on a piece of equipment to (increasingly) apps for smart phones (See Greater Insight D5.1). Regardless of the specific format and delivery mechanism, really useful performance support has the following characteristics:

Feature	Notes
Availability	Understand Audience. How and when to use it.
Specificity	
Practicality	
Economy	
Clarity	
Effectiveness	

Examples of Performance Support

Performance support can take many forms; common examples and their uses are listed below.

Type	Especially Good For
Checklist	Making sure all the key items in a procedure are included or completed. This is especially important when omission could lead to serious adverse consequences.
Step-by-Step Procedure	Making sure that a procedure is followed in the correct sequence. Especially valuable for complicated or rarely performed procedures or when someone is learning a new procedure.
Worksheet	Completing procedures that require calculations at various steps. A tax form is a good (albeit unpopular) example.
Flow Chart/If-Then Diagram	Guiding decision making or troubleshooting for well-defined problems that can be broken down into a series of defined choices. Helps ensure logical, step-by-step approach to problems.
"How-to" Video or Diagram	Showing exactly how to perform a specific procedure or where to locate a particular part or item; www.ehow.com, for example.

Script	Ensuring consistency, for example, to ensure that all customers receive the same marketing message or when conducting telephone surveys. Helpful for new employees learning company procedures.
Searchable Database	Providing rapid access to a large body of information. Online databases of products, models, and parts are good examples.
Help Desk/Access to Experts	Providing assistance with complex problems that using simpler job aids failed to solve.
Smart Phone App	Many of the above formats can be programmed as smart phone apps, which have the advantage of being available virtually any time and anywhere.

Checklist Masters

The airline industry has developed checklists for normal operations as well as for every conceivable emergency a flight crew might encounter (Gawande, 2009). Because time is often short and the stakes are high, these checklists have to be easy to understand and execute; they must contain all the essential items, but nothing extraneous. For that reason, airline checklists are extensively tested during development and revised as necessary. Applying these best practices to performance aids in training and development will increase their effectiveness and use.

When Is Performance Support Most Valuable?

Why This Exercise?

There are times when performance support is "nice to have" and other times when it is absolutely essential. To deploy resources effectively, we need to identify those situations in which support is especially important. This exercise provides an opportunity to think critically about when performance support is particularly valuable.

Instructions

1. Confer with your colleagues and generate a list of situations in which having performance support (job aids, checklists, step-by-step procedures, online databases, and so forth) is most valuable.
2. For each condition, provide an example—preferably from your program or organization.
3. We have provided one to help you start.

Performance support is most valuable when:	Example	Notes
The task is something you don't do very often.	Fixing a jammed copier.	It takes too long and costs too much to call a repairman each time. Step-by-step diagrams and instructions are on the machine and suffice most of the time; no training or special expertise is needed.

Performance support is most valuable when:	Example	Notes

Job Aids Are Not "Cheat Sheets"

The goal of providing performance support is to *make certain that*

by reducing the dependence on imperfect memory, especially when the stakes are high or the task is new or complex.

Job aids are often referred to as "cheat sheets," suggesting that it is somehow a sign of weakness or dishonesty to use them. As a passenger in an airplane, however, you wouldn't want your pilot to feel it was somehow cheating to use the checklist in an emergency and so decide to just "wing it."

As training professionals, we need to help people understand that using job aids is not only encouraged, but *it is expected*. Don't wait until the end of training to introduce a critical performance support tool. Make it an integral part of the training. Indeed, our colleague, Terrence Donahue, corporate director of training for Emerson, believes that you should design the job aid first and then structure the training to ensure that people learn how to use it.

> notes

Ideas into Action

❑ Review your program.

❑ If job aids or other kinds of performance support are provided, are they used as an integral part of the program?

❑ If not, build them into the practice sessions.

Do Job Aids Actually Enhance Performance?

What is the evidence that checklists, job aids, and other kinds of performance support actually improve performance enough to make it worth the effort to design and deploy them?

What Do You Think?

Could a simple job aid (a checklist) improve the success of surgery?

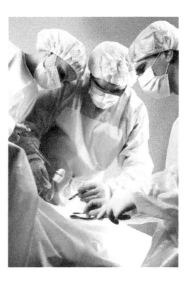

Here is the background: Surgeons and surgery teams are some of the most highly trained professionals in any field. They perform hundreds of procedures a year, so they have plenty of practice. Even so, mistakes happen; complications result.

So the World Health Organization sponsored the development of a simple, nineteen-item, three-part checklist that was to be completed before, during, and after each of the hundreds of different procedures performed in a typical hospital.

1. Do you think it had any effect?

2. If yes, how significant was it?

3. Was the effect seen across all hospitals or only in disadvantaged hospitals?

What the research showed:

Relevance to training and development:

 ## Is Training Really Necessary?

In D1, we concluded that training was an appropriate response when employees lacked the specific knowledge, skills, or experience to do a task. But even when this is true, is training always necessary?

 What Do You Think?

Are there ever times when a good job aid can eliminate the need for training? (Yes/No)
If so, what are they?

Job aids can replace the need for training when. . . .

Once we accept that the goal of training and development is to improve performance, rather than to deliver training *per se*, we will discover situations in which we can reduce or obviate the need for training through performance support. Recall that trusted advisors put their clients' needs (improved performance) ahead of their own (amount of training delivered).

Ideas into Action

- ❏ Challenge yourself and your team to identify areas in which you are providing training when the need could be met as well with a good job aid.
- ❏ Try to identify instances in which performance support could reduce the amount of training needed.
- ❏ Create the needed performance support and redirect training resources to more critical needs.

People as Performance Support

Sometimes, the support that is needed can only come from a human being. Examples include:

- ❏ _____
- ❏ _____
- ❏ _____

Greater Insight D5.2 lists some of the many ways that people can provide performance support. We have already discussed the critical support role that managers play in D4.

Kinds of Support Only People Can Provide

Coaching
Outstanding performers in every field have had coaches along the way—someone who can observe their performance and provide meaningful feedback on opportunities to improve. It is virtually impossible to become truly skilled without coaching. Depending on the skills to be mastered and the level of the trainee, potential coaches include peers, managers, and internal or external coaches.

Tricks of the Trade
Someone who has been doing a job for a while develops "tricks of the trade"—ways of performing tasks or skills that make them easier and more efficient to accomplish. Trainees may need to become proficient in the basics of performing the job before they can fully benefit from the performance tips of those skilled in the art. These performance tips are difficult to teach except in real time on the job. So being able to work alongside or observe a more experienced practitioner is often the best way to learn them.

Encouragement/ Moral Support
Sometimes the support that is needed is mainly in the form of encouragement or an expression of confidence. This is especially true when the learning curve is steep or the skill is difficult to master so that success is elusive for some time.

Expert Problem Solving
In many fields of knowledge work, some of the problems that new trainees will encounter are unique or particularly subtle or complex. In such situations, it is important to have access to much more experienced practitioners who have deep expertise and insight by dint of time and experience.

Mentoring	Mentoring is a long-term relationship between an advisor and advisee that focuses on career and professional development. Mentoring is a uniquely human kind of support that is especially important for developing research scientists and leaders.
Qualitative Assessment	When there is a strong qualitative component to the skills to be mastered—such as business writing, making sales or other presentations, leading meetings or teams, and so forth—then the performance support required needs to come from people who are able to judge the quality of the performance and provide advice and feedback. Consistency can be improved by providing rubrics for both the learners and their assessors.

For performance support from people to be effective, however, the people involved—whether they are peers, subject-matter experts, or managers—have to be prepared with the same care that would go into creating a job aid. Just because someone has been promoted to manager doesn't mean he or she knows how to provide meaningful support (Figure D5.2).

 What Do You Think?

Frequently, on-boarding programs for new employees include the assignment to work with or observe a more experienced employee perform the job. Talk to your colleagues and answer the three questions on the next page.

What is good about such assignments?

What is sub-optimal?

How can the value of such experiences be improved?

"Keep up the good work, whatever it is, whoever you are."

Figure D5.2. Managers Also Need Performance Support

"Implementing any kind of
performance support system . . .
can have a significant effect on user
performance and attitudes."

—Frank Nguyen, in *Job Aids and
Performance Support*

Peer Coaches

Peer coaches (sometimes called "learning buddies") can be valuable sources of accountability as well as support; they are under-utilized by most training departments. Peer coaches aren't just for new hires. General Electric found peer support to be of value even in their most senior executive leadership programs: "When the leadership teams share their development needs with each other and use the coaching model, they often find three things: (1) they have ___Similar issues___, (2) they get great ___improvement sugestion___ from each other, and (3) they get _____ from each other to improve" (Sharkey, 2003).

Of course, peer coaching can also be "the blind leading the blind" if people don't recognize their limits. So it is important to provide guidelines for peer coaching and to ensure that there is a backup mechanism if they are out of their depth.

BOTTOM LINE

Sometimes people are the best—or only—means of providing the needed performance support. To achieve the greatest value from people as performance support, both the trainees and those providing support must be prepared. In other words, you need to provide performance support for those providing performance support.

Ideas into Action

❑ Review your program. Are there unfulfilled opportunities to provide performance support through people that would significantly enhance performance?

❑ If so, figure out who can provide that support and what support *he or she* will need to be successful.

❑ Provide it.

Design (or Enhance) Performance Support

Why This Exercise?

This exercise is an opportunity to convert D5 concepts into action and practice using a job aid for designing performance support.

Instructions

1. Complete the performance support planner below. It may help to find a partner and "interview" each other using the planner questions and the Checklist for D5 in the Appendix.

2. Start with the end in mind, that is, by anticipating the kinds of difficulties or memory lapses participants are likely to run into when they try to apply what they learned for the first few times. [If your program has been given

before, interview some prior participants to see what challenges they faced where performance support would have helped.]

3. Then consider what kind of support would be most effective (step-by-step procedure, checklist, database, expert advice, etc.).

4. Decide how best to deliver it to ensure that support is available at the time and place it is needed. It may make sense to provide more than one means of access (paper and online, for example). Try to think "outside the box" and consider novel solutions, but don't overcomplicate it; if a simple posted procedure will suffice, use it.

5. Work with your colleagues and/or the instructor to help each other develop a really valuable addition to your program.

6. Be prepared to share good ideas with the whole group.

Performance Support Planner *"Decision tree to be use"*

What are people most likely to have trouble remembering or performing?

- ~~below~~ verbalization
- New Data
- Clear pt type.

What kind of support will be most helpful?

- ☐ Checklist
- ☒ Step-by-step procedure
- ☒ Worksheet
- ☒ Flow chart/if-then diagram
- ☒ "How-to" video or diagram

☑ Script

❑ Searchable database

❑ Help desk/access to experts

❑ Other: _____

Where will they be at the time?

At the POA.
Press Work.

Given the above, what delivery system(s) make the most sense?

☒ Paper-based job aid

☒ Online

❑ Smart phone app

☒ Posted instructions

❑ Other: _Pull through → accountability among peers_
Call each other for feedback.

Taken together, describe the performance support you could create that will help ensure everyone is able to perform on the job satisfactorily after training:

Reflect and Plan

Why This Exercise?

This is an opportunity for you to reflect on and elaborate the key concepts and personal "takeaways" from our discussion of D5.

Instructions

1. Look back over this section and your notes.
2. Add any key insights to the D5 branch of the 6Ds Mind Map.
3. Draw any relevant connections between D5 concepts and other branches.
4. Extend your Two Questions Mind Map by adding any associations that come to mind between D5 and the "Can I?" and "Will I?" questions.
5. Consider what actions you could take to apply D5 to create additional value from training. Record your ideas for action on the Road Map to Results.
6. Transfer one or two of your best ideas from your personal maps to the community maps on the wall.

- Knowing that they do not have to remember everything and that assistance is available helps learners answer the "Can I?" question in the affirmative.

- Post-training performance support helps people utilize their training more successfully, which increases both the participants' and managers' satisfaction with the outcome.

- Performance support can take many forms.

- Key features of effective support include availability at the time and place it is needed; clarity; practical focus; effectiveness; and just enough detail to accomplish the task.

- For some tasks, a good job aid is all that is needed; training may be unnecessary.

- Introduce and use job aids during the training, not as an afterthought.

- Sometimes only people can provide the kind of support needed. Those who will be providing support should be prepared to do so effectively.

- Performance support is part of the complete learning experience; every training design should include an assessment of the kinds of support needed and a plan for using the best mechanisms to deliver it.

D6 Document Results

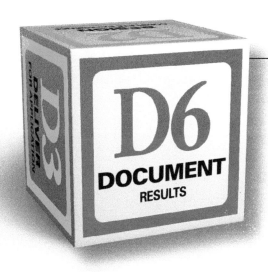

"You, your leaders, and your investors are interested in learning only insofar as it improves performance and gets business results."

—Dulworth and Bordonaro, *Corporate Learning*

Why Document Results?

What Do You Think?

Is it important for training and development departments to document the results of training?

   If so, why?

   Confer with your colleagues and be prepared to share your answers and rationale.

The Manager's Dilemma

Business managers are charged with using the company's resources in a way that maximizes the long-term benefit for the shareholders, customers, and employees. Because resources are finite—even in a highly successful firm—managers must make hard choices among sometimes very different kinds of initiatives. For example:

❑ Fund a risky, but promising, research project that won't pay off for several years

❑ Hire more sales representatives to boost short-term sales

❑ Increase the marketing budget

❑ Invest more in training

Moreover, they know that their decisions will be reviewed and potentially criticized. Therefore, they favor investments that are backed by good business cases. They want to know whether or not similar investments in the past were successful.

 ## What Do You Think?

If you were about to invest a sizable portion of your personal retirement savings, which would you be more likely to choose?

❏ A fund that never issued any performance analyses, but just said "trust us, we are doing great" or

❏ A fund that has a strong record of delivering results and that regularly reports its performance.

notes

Application to Training and Development

The analogy to training and development is clear. Managers will be more willing to invest in training—especially when funds are tight—if we have established a strong record of performance and report results on an ongoing basis.

D6
DOCUMENT
RESULTS

Continuous Improvement

The other key reason to evaluate training outcomes is to drive continuous improvement.

What Do You Think?

Imagine that you are the catapult captain for the City of Syracuse in 212 BC. The Roman fleet, under the command of their best admiral, Marcellus, has sailed into the harbor and is preparing to sack your city. Your job is to sink their ships with boulders from your catapult before they can proceed. You can adjust the direction, elevation (angle), and power of the catapult. What do you need to know after each shot?

> "The ability to learn faster than your competitors may be the only sustainable competitive advantage."
>
> —Arie de Gues, Strategic Planner, Royal Dutch Shell

Application to Training and Development

In D4, we introduced the PDCA/Deming Cycle for continuous improvement (Figure D6.1).

As you recall, the check step—analyzing the actual results compared to the goal—is vital. If you don't assess the results, then you don't have any idea whether changes you have made were improvements or, in fact, made things worse.

Many learning organizations introduce changes in training design, delivery, or technology in an effort to improve results, but then don't measure the relevant outcomes. Change is not necessarily improvement; you have to evaluate and document results to know whether you have made things better, worse, or had no effect.

D6
DOCUMENT
RESULTS

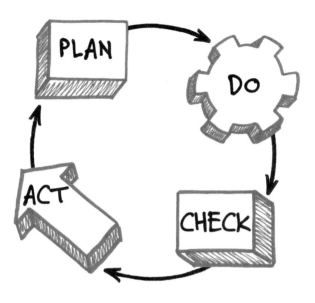

Figure D6.1. The PDCA/ Deming Cycle

D6 and the Two Questions

Training produces business results only when participants answer "Yes" to both the "Can I?" and "Will I?" questions. The only way to know their answers is to gather evidence that the training is being applied on the job and is improving performance. If you are not seeing the expected outcomes, then you have to do a root cause analysis to find out where the process broke down.

While it's useful to ask people at the end of training whether they feel prepared and motivated to use what they learn (see D3), that isn't sufficient because: _____.

Not All "Results" Matter

Just because something can be quantified and made into cool charts and graphs doesn't mean it is useful to prove or improve training's value.

You Be the Judge

"Not everything that can be counted counts."

—Alfred Einstein

Why This Exercise?

The purpose of this exercise is to help clarify what we mean by "results" and to drive home the point that many of the measures most frequently reported by training departments miss the mark.

Your Turn

D6
DOCUMENT
RESULTS

Instructions

1. Watch the mini role play.
2. Decide which chief learning officer is most likely to have his or her budget request approved.
3. Explain why.

Means vs. Ends

Training departments need to quantify costs and activities in order to manage their operations. It's essential to know things like the number of trainees, the cost per person, number of e-learning courses completed, hours of training, classroom utilization, and so forth. But these are measures of *activity* (means); they are not the *results* (ends) for which training was funded.

"If you are spending just $1 on training but getting no business value in return, then you are over-spending."

—Van Adelsberg and Trolley, *Running Training Like a Business*

One of the most common errors that training departments make is to report measures of means as if they were outcomes (ends). The number of people trained, for example, is meaningless in the absence of a measure of training effectiveness.

 What Do You Think?

To be sure the difference between means and ends is clear, please indicate which of the following are primarily measures of *means* (inputs) and which are measures of ends (the results that the business expects in return for its investment).

Means	Ends	Measure
❏	❏	Number of trainees for a given program or period
❏	❏	Reduced number of data-entry errors
❏	❏	Number of e-learning modules completed
❏	❏	Improved customer satisfaction
❏	❏	Cost of the new-hire training program
❏	❏	Shorter time to productivity for new hires
❏	❏	Number of new safety training programs developed
❏	❏	Reduced accidents and downtime

Just as it is meaningless to report the number of people trained without a concomitant measure of whether the training improved performance, it is meaningless to report a change in cost without simultaneously assessing relevant results.

For example:

❏ If you reduced the cost of training by 25 percent by using more e-learning AND the effectiveness was the same or greater, then you deserve

_____ .

❏ However, if you reduced the cost by 25 percent but the effectiveness declined by 33 percent, then you deserve _____ .

D6
DOCUMENT
RESULTS

If all you know is that you reduced cost by 25 percent, but you have no idea whether the results are the same, better, or worse, you do not know what you're doing.

Ideas into Action

- ❏ Review the three most recent reports your department submitted to management.
- ❏ Are the measures reported mostly measures of means or do they also report assessment of the ends for which the training was requested?
- ❏ If they are only measures of means, correct the situation.

Guiding Principles

Training and development covers a vast range of topics and skills even within a single company. It should be obvious that no one measure or evaluation approach will work across courses as diverse as on-boarding, strategic planning, software programming, sales basics, plant safety, leadership, and so on.

There is, however, a small set of guiding principles that can be used to help design and assess the quality of program evaluation across the whole breadth of training and development.

An effective evaluation is

- ❏ _____ to the program's purpose
- ❏ _____ to the stakeholders
- ❏ _____ to the decision-makers
- ❏ _____ in its use of resources

"I don't know a CEO who doesn't love numbers."

—Jeffrey Silverman, CEO, Ply-Gen

D6
DOCUMENT
RESULTS

What's the relevance result measure ??

Relevant

The first and critical criterion for a meaningful measure is that it must be directly *relevant* to the program's purpose. That is, there must be a clear and unambiguous connection between the goals defined by the sponsor in D1 and what is measured and reported in D6 (Figure D6.2).

Figure D6.2. D6 Must Measure the Outcomes Defined in D1

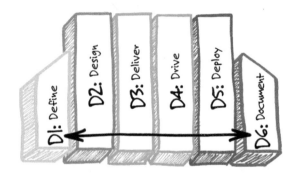

Immediate post-class reaction scores (Kirkpatrick Level 1)—no matter how glowing they are—fail the test of relevance. Learner satisfaction is not the reason that training is funded.

Coincidentally, Level 1 scores do not correlate with either the amount learned or whether it will be used. Hence, relying solely on Level 1 scores can even lead to misguided decisions. (See Greater Insight D6.1: A Little Evaluation Can Be a Dangerous Thing.)

Start with the Claim

To ensure that measures are relevant, ask yourself: What did the training promise? Remember that, in D1, we asked you to succinctly state the promise (claim) of your training program. Any time that we agree to provide training, we

GREATER INSIGHT D6.1

A Little Evaluation Can Be a Dangerous Thing

A technology company was thinking of firing one of its instructors because he consistently received poor ratings on an end-of-course questionnaire. So they asked Neil Rackham, best-selling author of *SPIN Selling*, for advice.

When Rackham re-ranked the instructors based on learning gains for students, rather than popularity, the results were startling. The poorly rated trainer was actually among the best on staff. "In the end," said Rackham, "Level 1 smile sheets had given management the exact wrong impression" (quoted by Boehle, 2006).

What's the danger of relying only on Level 1 reactions?

Many end-of-course evaluations are essentially popularity ratings. Things that make an instructor effective in terms of ultimate performance—such as requiring role plays, challenging participants to think, and giving candid feedback—do not necessarily make him or her popular.

Conversely, trainers can do things that boost their reaction ratings that may actually diminish learning effectiveness—for example, let people out early, skip unpopular exercises, grade easier, etc.

The point is that "what you measure is what you get." And getting the highest possible reaction ratings does not necessarily equate to gaining the maximum possible value from training.

make the claim: "Give us your people, your time, and your support, and we will improve their performance in [insert outcome here]." A *relevant* measure is one that provides data to back up the claim.

Learn by Analogy

Propose the relevant measure(s) to support each of the claims below.

In Order to Claim That	You Need to Measure
"Our appliance uses one-third less electricity than our competitor's."	
"The new maintenance procedure takes less time but produces the same quality."	
"The new return policy has increased customer loyalty."	
"Our leadership development program helps create more effective leaders."	

Don't Confuse What with How

As the above examples illustrate, when a claim is clearly stated, *what* needs to be measured is pretty obvious. Notice, however, that we did not say *how* electrical consumption or quality or loyalty or effectiveness would be measured. *How* you would actually evaluate each claim requires:

a. _____

b. _____

One of the most common errors that learning organizations make is jumping straight to *how* to measure results without first gaining agreement on *what* needs to be measured and how it is defined.

"If you don't measure it, you can't manage it."

BOTTOM LINE

Always start with *what* needs to be measured to evaluate training's effectiveness and make sure that all the stakeholders are defining it in the same way.

Your Turn

Clarify the Relevant Measures for Your Program

Why This Exercise?

A clear and unambiguous statement of the program's promise (claim) is the starting point for effective evaluation. The purpose of this exercise is to help you clarify relevant measures for your program's promise.

A *relevant* measure is one that provides the information necessary to support or refute the claim. While there are an essentially infinite number of

D6
DOCUMENT
RESULTS

things that could be measured, there are a limited number of *kinds* of data and ways to collect it. You may find it helpful to refer to the listing in the Appendix.

Instructions

1. Review what you defined as the promise of your training program in D1.
2. Insert it into the claim statement below.
3. Then propose a relevant measure and its definition.
4. Discuss with a colleague and be prepared to share with the group.

Claim Statement

"The ___*POA E*___ [name of program] together with on-the-job support from managers, will ___*Acederate trials*___ [insert verb such as increase, decrease, accelerate, achieve, etc.] by ___*def and pull through appropiate pt type* ___.
[complete how much by when if that has been discussed with the sponsor and defined as part of the agreement].

Therefore, the relevant measure(s) of this program's effectiveness are _____
___*In respect fully number of differenciates pt type and*___.

Example: "The on-boarding program, in concert with support from supervisors, will produce 'client-ready' customer service representatives who are able to perform independently to departmental standards within twenty-three days of beginning the program. Therefore, the relevant measure is the number of days until the representative consistently achieves a satisfactory score on ratings of randomly monitored calls."

Timing

Deciding *when* to evaluate is almost as important as deciding *what* to evaluate (see Greater Insight D6.2: When to Measure). You need to wait long enough for on-the-job results to become apparent, but not so long that they are completely obscured by other factors. You also want to evaluate as early as possible so that you can make adjustments to the program if necessary.

> ## GREATER INSIGHT D6.2
>
> ### When to Measure
>
> Deciding *when* to collect the data is almost as important as deciding what to collect.
>
> Since D6 is about documenting business-relevant results, that virtually excludes any data collected at the end of instruction, since the participants will not yet have *done* anything that would generate business value. Participants need time to *transfer* their new knowledge and skills

to their jobs and *apply* them long enough to improve performance. Relevant results can only be collected after enough time has elapsed for this to occur.

For some kinds of training—such as customer service, manufacturing, or computer skills—demonstrable improvement might be manifest within days. For others—such as strategic selling, management, or leadership training—it might be weeks or months before the desired effects can be documented.

The general principle is to assess the results at the earliest point at which the outcomes of interest will be evident. The longer you wait, the more extraneous factors impact the results. For programs that require a long time before results are evident—and which are thus confounded by non-training factors—look for leading indicators.

Leading indicators are measures that, while not strictly results themselves, are good predictors of future impact. The idea comes from Kaplan and Norton's concept of the Balanced Scorecard (1996). For example, a company that is losing customers may still be doing well financially *today*, but the loss of customers is a *leading indicator* of trouble ahead. The most common leading indicator of training's success is performance of the vital behaviors in the second quadrant of the Outcomes Planning Wheel, because these behaviors are what lead to improved business results.

Focus on *leading indicators* that the program is working—usually behaviors—as opposed to the ultimate results (which often have multiple contributing factors; see Figure D6.3).

Figure D6.3. More Effective Actions Are Leading Indicators of Future Resuts

LEADING INDICATORS:

Successful training & development → More effective or efficient actions & behaviors → Improved business results

Examples of Leading Indicators

Type of Program	Ultimate Goal	Leading Indicator
First time mngr.	Improve retention	Employee satisf.
IVA	Increased sales	Frequency and effect. of use
Safe drive skills.	Fewer accid/ violations	Observation of safe driving

Isolating the Effects of Training

Isolating the effects of training from the effects of the transfer climate requires very sophisticated trial designs and statistical analysis. In our view, it is not a productive exercise.

What Do You Think?

What percent of your success in business is the result of learning to read?

_____ percent.

   Asking people to estimate the percent that training contributed to a business result is equally impossible. It is important for learners and managers to agree that the training was a catalyst in achieving the results, but trying to calculate how much is, in our opinion, a fool's errand and not very credible.

Share the Credit

We have said that managers are a frequent cause of training failure; they are also an indispensable component of training's success. Therefore, *always acknowledge the role of managers in any successful training outcome.*

Credible

The second criterion of an effective evaluation is that it is *credible*, that is, it is believed and trusted by the key stakeholders. Credibility is mainly about *how* the evaluation is conducted—the way in which the data were collected, from whom and by whom, and how much there is.

What Do You Think?

Rate the credibility of the following statements:

1. The government-controlled news agency released a poll of seven members of the cabinet who gave the prime minister uniformly high marks.
   ❏ Not credible   ❏ Suspect   ❏ Credible   ❏ Highly credible

2. An independent polling organization, based on telephone interviews of one thousand randomly selected voters, reported that Candidate A had a 56 to 39 percent lead over Candidate B, with 5 percent undecided and a margin of error of plus or minus 3 percent.
   ❏ Not credible   ❏ Suspect   ❏ Credible   ❏ Highly credible

3. A week after the "Consultative Selling Skills" program, we conducted a Level 2 analysis of learning by polling all fifty-eight participants about how much they learned. The nineteen who responded gave the program a 4.2 out of 5 rating, indicating that we achieved 84 percent of the learning objectives.
   ❏ Not credible   ❏ Suspect   ❏ Credible   ❏ Highly credible

4. After the "Better Business Writing" program, we submitted before and after writing samples from the participants to three independent raters from our communications department. The raters were asked to score the samples on organization, clarity, grammar, and punctuation using a standard rubric. Raters did not know which were the before and which were the after samples or who wrote them. In eighteen of twenty cases, the post-training samples were rated significantly better than the pre-training samples. The greatest gains were in clarity and organization.
   ❏ Not credible   ❏ Suspect   ❏ Credible   ❏ Highly credible

D6
DOCUMENT
RESULTS

Based on your reactions to the above, list some of the key characteristics that you took into consideration in deciding how much credibility you afforded the results.

Key factors that I consider in deciding how much credence to give information include:

❏ _____

❏ _____

❏ _____

Application to Training and Development

For evaluations to convincingly demonstrate training's value, the measures reported must be *credible* as well as *relevant*. If the sponsors don't trust the data, they won't trust the conclusions. Take steps to enhance credibility. For example, if the sponsor insists on analysis of the financial return as a criterion for success, ask the finance department to do the analysis rather than doing it yourself.

For additional information on reliability, validity, and bias, consult experts in your company, such as your market researchers, or an authoritative text on evaluation such as Babbie (2010) or Russ-Eft and Preskill (2009).

"Credibility is one of the hardest attributes to earn. And it is the most fragile of human qualities."

—Kouzes and Posner, *The Leadership Challenge*

D6
DOCUMENT
RESULTS

Compelling

The only reason to measure anything is to *inform action*.

The third guiding principle for evaluation is that the results should *compel* managers to take action, such as expanding the program, continuing it, or cancelling it altogether.

The magnitude of the value created needs to be big enough to capture management's attention *and* the results have to be presented in a way that motivates management to act. In other words, results must be *marketed*, not just reported.

The Power of Stories

You know how valuable stories can be in teaching. But should stories be part of a presentation to hard-boiled business executives?

What Do You Think?

Three different groups of MBA students were given the same information. The first group received a verbal description that contained facts and figures. The second group received the same information, but presented in the form of charts and tables. The third group received the same information, but presented as the story of a little old winemaker.

"Stories are easy to remember, probably because they are how we remember."

—Daniel Pink,
A Whole New Mind

❑ Which group do you think remembered the most?

story

❑ Which presentation did they find the most credible and compelling?

story

BOTTOM LINE

Even if you have great quantitative data, include stories that illustrate how trainees are using what they learned on the job and obtaining results. "Concrete and vivid stories exert extraordinary influence because they transport people out of the role of critic and into the role of participant" (Patterson, Grenny, Maxfield, McMillan, & Switzler, 2008, p. 61).

Ideas into Action

❑ When you communicate results to management, supplement your tables, charts, and graphs with stories that illustrate the key findings. They will be remembered long after the charts are forgotten.

Check Your Understanding

Why This Exercise?

This exercise provides an opportunity for you to check your understanding to be sure that you have internalized the guiding principles.

Instructions

1. Read the brief evaluation summaries below.
2. Confer with your colleagues.
3. Rate each evaluation summary against the first three guiding principles. Does it satisfy all three, two, one, or none?
4. Be prepared to discuss your thinking.

Summary	Scorecard
We conducted a program on managing employee relationships for front-line supervisors. The goal of the program was to improve employee engagement and reduce grievances by teaching supervisors how to give more constructive feedback—both positive and negative. We trained 385 supervisors in groups of 20 to 25 to ensure active participation. Overall, the supervisors rated the program 4.85 of 5.0, which compares favorably to the industry average of 4.2. A typical comment was: "Great program, I really learned a lot!"	❏ Relevant ❏ Credible ❏ Compelling

Summary	Scorecard
The objective of the "How to Handle Objections" course was to increase sales by improving salespeople's ability to handle objections. We reasoned, therefore, that the real measure of success would be an increase in sales. So we asked each salesperson to estimate how much his or her sales had increased since the program. Salespeople estimate a 36 percent increase—or just over $2 million—in the three months since the training. Since the cost of the program was less than $200,000, that is an ROI of 900 percent.	❏ Relevant ❏ Credible ❏ Compelling
The "Safety Is Everyone's Responsibility" program is designed to reduce injuries, lost time, and citations for safety violations by empowering every employee to stop an unsafe practice by any other employee. Six months after the program and reinforcement activities, the number of OSHA citations for unsafe practices has been reduced by half; reportable accidents have decreased 11 percent; and there has been no lost time due to injury since the program. When polled, both supervisors and employees credit the program with making a real difference in their work practices.	☒ Relevant ☒ Credible ❏ Compelling

Ideas into Action

❏ Review your most recent program evaluation against the three guiding principles.

❏ If it did not satisfy all three, take corrective action.

Efficient

The final guiding principle is that evaluations should be efficient. That is, they should use the minimum amount of time and money necessary to answer the questions:

❏ Is the training producing the results for which it was designed?

❏ If not, where is the process breaking down?

❏ How can it be made even more effective?

Two keys to improving the efficiency of evaluation are to:

❏ Collect only the data needed to make an informed decision and

❏ Use technology to automate the process when appropriate

IMPORTANT: Don't bother trying to improve efficiency unless

_____.

Doing the wrong thing at low cost is not efficient!

"What is troubling is not just being average but settling for it."

—Atul Gawande, _Better: A Surgeon's Notes on Performance_

notes

Support Continuous Improvement

Evaluation should always serve to _____ as well as to _____ value creation. Continuous improvement requires:

❑ Knowing how close you came to the target
❑ Actively seeking out weak points and opportunities for improvement

While it is tempting to only look for "good news" when conducting an evaluation, progressive learning professionals also include questions and gather data on weaknesses and points of failure.

In *Telling Training's Story* (2006), Rob Brinkerhoff summarized his Success Case Method, which includes surveying participants at an appropriate interval after training to determine who achieved success and who did not, and then interviewing a sample of each (Figure D6.4).

Figure D6.4. Brinkerhoff's Success Case Method

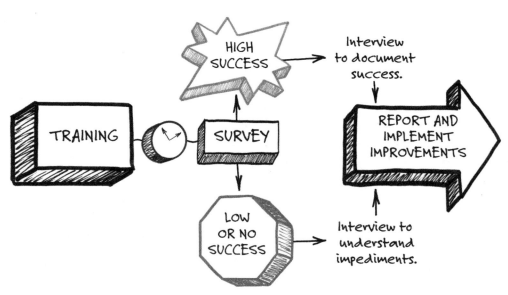

The purpose of interviewing the low- or no-success participants is to "find out what went wrong: what got in the way of using the training, and why it was not productively used or used at all" (p. 126).

Asking participants "What can be improved?" at the end of training is useful, but not sufficient. More often than not, the real impediments to transfer are in the _____, and that insight can only be gained by evaluating transfer after days or weeks back on the job.

The results of your evaluation—good or bad—must be honestly and courageously reported to management, together with specific recommendations to improve future programs and iterations.

Ideas into Action

- ❏ Review your three most recent program evaluations.
- ❏ Do they provide guidance on how to improve both the program and the transfer climate?
- ❏ If not, implement a plan to collect data several weeks post-training to understand whether or not the training is being applied and why.

Your Turn

Convert Learning into Action

Why This Exercise?

The purpose of this exercise is to give you a chance to practice applying D6 principles to the program you brought to the workshop while you have professional colleagues and the facilitators available to help.

Instructions

1. Complete the Evaluation Planner below for your program.
2. Then use the Evaluation Checklist in the Appendix to look for opportunities to strengthen your design.
3. Make notes about actions you need to take, for example, to obtain assistance with measurement, explore alternatives, or secure permission to access data.

Evaluation Planner

Name of program to be evaluated: _____

Concise statement of program's promise:

Relevant outcomes that must be measured to support the claim (focus on leading indicators):

Mechanism(s) for collecting data:

❏ Surveys

❏ Interviews

❏ Review company records

❏ Observations

❏ Focus groups

❏ Evaluate work product(s)

❏ Other: _____

How will you identify opportunities for improvement?

Timing (How long between the training and the evaluation?)

"You can't be subtle or naïve if you want managers to pay attention to your metrics. Most reports from development are too long, too dull, and just plain uninteresting."

—John Sullivan, in *The Future of Executive Development*

Marketing Your Value

It doesn't matter how great your results are; if no one knows about them, your contributions will be undervalued and underappreciated. For training and development to be a respected business partner, we need to do a better job of marketing our contributions.

The first step is to decide who needs to know and what messages will resonate with which audiences. For example, management will want to hear examples of how the training is producing business-relevant results. Future trainees will be most interested in examples of how the training benefitted past participants.

Once you know your results and the core message for each audience, then use as many communication opportunities and vehicles as you can to put the word out. Don't tell them just once. Take an example from McDonald's: they keep reminding you that they sell fast food, even though you already know that. The rule of thumb is that a customer has to hear a message six times before it really sticks. Choose a few core messages and weave them into all your presentations and interactions with business leaders. Equip everyone on the team to help reinforce the key themes of training's value.

Reflect and Plan

Why This Exercise?

This exercise is an opportunity to reflect on D6, connect key ideas from other parts of the program, and plan for transfer.

Instructions

1. Look back over this section and your notes.

2. Add ideas and links to your mind maps.

3. Consider the most important actions you can take to strengthen the evaluation and reporting of results in your organization. Write them on your Road Map.

4. Transfer one or two of your best ideas to the community maps.

- Training departments must document results in order to *prove* that value was created as well as to *improve* future offerings.
- Measures of means—like the cost of delivery, number of programs and trainees, etc.—are meaningless unless you also have true outcome measures.
- Reaction scores, and even assessments of the amount learned, are not the results the business is looking for in return for its investment.
- The guiding principles for an evaluation are that it must be
  - Relevant
  - Credible
  - Compelling
  - And, once all three of those are satisfied, efficient.
- In developing an evaluation strategy, always clarify *what* needs to be measured before worrying about *how*.

Getting Your Money's Worth

"We must take responsibility for our professional growth and aggressively pursue it."

—Kevin Washburn, *The Architecture of Learning*

You and your organization will benefit from this workshop only to the extent that you transfer what you have learned to your work and apply the 6Ds principles in ways that improve training's effectiveness.

What Do You Think?

Suppose you were a manager who had sent two employees to training.

Amelia completed all the required preparation and met with you to discuss what you wanted her to get out of the workshop. During the training, she participated actively and was a positive contributor to the group's discussions. She felt she got a lot out of the session and that what she learned was relevant and practical to her work. She set a SMART goal for applying what she learned and was enthused about achieving it. When she got back to work, however, a lot of tasks had piled up and there were some urgent deadlines, so she set her workbook aside with the intention of getting back to it. It has now been two months since training and she still has not started on her objective from the workshop.

Bedelia attended the same training. She completed the preparatory work and had a short email exchange with you about your goals for her attendance. She is rather shy, and although she paid attention, she mostly listened during the group exercises and never volunteered to lead her table group. At the conclusion of the workshop, she also set a goal for herself to apply what she learned. The day after the workshop, she sent you a copy of her goal and asked for input. She also asked for time at the next team meeting to summarize her key takeaways with the rest of the team. Over the next couple of weeks, you noticed her sharing concepts from the training with her co-workers in meetings and casual conversations. She kept a learning journal and would periodically record opportunities she had identified to apply the learning and her reflections on her progress. Two months after the training, she sent you a short summary of what she had accomplished, where she ran into obstacles, what she had learned in the process, and her recommendations going forward.

1. Who do you think learned more during the workshop?

2. Who do you think generated the greatest value for the company?

3. What were some of the key actions this person took to create more value?

4. Who would you be more likely to send to a future learning opportunity?

Maximize Your Return

You have already invested two days of your valuable time. To be sure you maximize the return on that investment:

1. **Set a goal for applying what you have learned.**

   People who set goals for themselves are more likely to achieve them, especially if they share the goal with others. Review your Road Map to Results to help you recall opportunities you have identified throughout the workshop. Choose the one thing you could accomplish by applying the 6Ds that would have the greatest value for you, your program's participants, and your organization.

2. **Teach others.**

   When you get back to work, share what you have learned with others. You know from experience that the best way to learn something well is to teach it to others. There is solid brain research to support this. Every time you explain a concept, relate an example, or retell a story—a process known as *elaborative rehearsal*—you strengthen the neural pathways and connections to it, making it easier to recall and apply in the future. Teaching needn't involve a formal presentation (although we have included slides in the toolkit that you can use to present a brief overview); just bringing up relevant concepts from the workshop in meetings and conversations accomplishes the same end. It helps both you and others succeed.

   Preparing an Elevator Speech (page 209) is a good place to start.

"The best development goal is one that will bring high value both to your business and to you."

—Calhoun Wick, *The Learning Edge*

3. Seek opportunities to apply the 6Ds.

Learning is most fragile when it is new. The sooner you can use what you learned, the less likely you are to forget it. Try to find an opportunity to apply the two fundamental questions and a concept from each of the 6Ds to your work over the next eight weeks. As a personal challenge and to enjoy a sense of accomplishment, see how quickly you can complete the 6Ds Challenge Self-Report Card below.

6Ds Challenge Self-Report Card

To reinforce your learning and improve later recall, see how quickly you can apply a principle from each D and the two fundamental questions in the course of your work. Use the self-report card below to help you keep track.

☑	Discipline	Date Used	Context and Notes on Outcome
❏	D1: Define		
❏	D2: Design		
❏	D3: Deliver		
❏	D4: Drive		
❏	D5: Deploy		
❏	D6: Document		
❏	Can I?		
❏	Will I?		

Set a Specific Goal

Why This Exercise?

You will be more likely to produce value if you have a specific objective in mind. This exercise provides you with the opportunity to set a personal goal for applying concepts and tools from the 6Ds to your ongoing work as a learning professional.

Instructions

1. Review the ideas that you have recorded in your personal 6Ds Road Map to Results as well as others' ideas from the group map.
2. Pick one specific thing you want to accomplish by applying 6Ds principles and/or best practices you learned from your colleagues.
3. Write a draft goal using the suggested format below. You may find it helpful to refer to the sample goals on pages 214 and 215.
4. Share your goal with others and obtain their input.
5. Transfer your final objective to the Goal Form at the end of the workbook and turn it in before you leave.

Your Draft Goal

In the next eight weeks, I will . . . (describe what you will accomplish)

So that . . . (describe the payoff or benefit)

Indicators of my progress will include . . . (What will be the evidence of your progress and success?)

Your Turn

Prepare an Elevator Speech

Why This Exercise?

When you return to the office tomorrow, your manager and co-workers are likely to ask you about this workshop. If you have a succinct, well-thought-out "elevator speech," you will be able to seize the opportunity to demonstrate your ability to learn and grow.

The concept of an elevator speech originated at Xerox years ago. The idea was that if a senior manager asked you on an elevator, "So what is this idea of yours?" you would have roughly thirty seconds to explain it. If you could quickly and clearly articulate your key points, you might gain a convert; if you couldn't clearly make your case before the doors opened again, you lost a golden opportunity.

Instructions

1. If you finish writing your goal while others are still working, prepare your elevator speech by answering the four questions below.
2. If time permits, practice your speech with a partner.
3. If you do not have time to create your speech now, do so on the trip home. The time you spend thinking about the key points you want to communicate will be repaid many times over.

Elevator Speech
1. The most important/striking/insightful/valuable (pick one) thing I learned was: *dif ~~before~~ Activ. to ~~detwsch~~ help learn / Define goal.*
2. I am going to capitalize on this learning by: *POA*
3. The benefit for our organization will be: *Engageing our new TBM during training.*
4. I'll need the following help to make this happen: *Other RFST & In house trainer*

Consider asking learners in your own programs to prepare elevator speeches. It will help them reinforce their own learning, and also will benefit the training department. Management will have a more positive impression of the value of training when participants are able to concisely summarize the value and benefit of what they learned, rather than just commenting on the facilitator's style, the venue, or what they had to eat.

Gain Valuable Feedforward

Executive Coach Marshall Goldsmith developed the concept of feedforward as a rapid way to capture a lot of ideas and suggestions that are focused on the future (as opposed to "feedback," which focuses on the past).

Why This Exercise?

This exercise gives you the opportunity to tap the expertise and experience of the other learning professionals in the room on how you might accomplish your goal. It is also an opportunity to learn the feedforward method, which can be used as a valuable concluding exercise in many kinds of training.

Instructions

Your goal is to talk to as many people and gather as many ideas as you can in the time allotted. Here's how:

1. Stand up.
2. Find another person.
3. Share your goal.
4. Ask for one "feedforward" idea (something you could do).
5. Say "thank you." (Don't say whether you like the idea or not.)
6. Trade roles.
7. Find another partner.

8. Repeat the process as many times as you can in the allotted time.

9. Keep score by making a tick mark below for each idea you get and each idea you give during the exercise.

Feedforward Scorecard

Number of Ideas Given	Number of Ideas Received

Feedforward Ideas to Consider

Now What?

Now it is up to you.

Become a role model for learning transfer.

Teach others, look for opportunities, and continue your learning journey; we'll be here to help.

We look forward to hearing about your achievements.

SUMMING UP

- Any training and development program—including this one—delivers value only when its teachings are transferred and applied to the business of the business.

- Strong, well-articulated goals are more likely to produce results than weak or vague ones.

- People have a "golden opportunity" when they first return to work to communicate their intentions, explain the value of applying what they learned, and ask for assistance.

- Helping participants prepare an elevator speech is good for the participants and good for the training department.

- Now it is up to you to take what you learned and convert it into value for your organization and your career. Best wishes for great success!

Sample Goals from This Workshop

Here are examples of a goal for each of the Ds to help you think about what you might want to accomplish and how to describe it:

D1: Define Business Outcomes

In the next eight weeks, I will make sure I understand the business drivers and required behaviors following the XYZ Program by interviewing key stakeholders using the 6Ds Planning Wheel.

I will summarize the results of those discussions and check for understanding so that I am certain I know what is expected from the program and that it is focused on the most important business needs.

Evidence of my progress will include completed interviews, my Planning Wheel, and a written agreement with the sponsors.

D2: Design the Complete Experience

In the next eight weeks, I will revise and implement an improved process for inviting people to participate in the ABC Program so that they are more motivated to attend and so that the expectations are clear.
Indicators of my progress will include these things:

❏ Defining a new process and having it approved

❏ Having senior vice president sign the invitation

❏ Making sure the invitation states clear expectations for application on the job

❏ Including examples of success by prior participants

❏ Having former participants agree the new invitation is a much clearer and more motivating message than they had received

D3: Deliver for Application

In the next eight weeks, I will review and revise the end-of-course assessment to ensure that it tests participants' ability to *apply* the course material and not merely play it back.

Indicators of my progress will include:

❏ Scoring the cognitive level of all our current test questions according to Bloom's taxonomy

❏ Replacing or rewriting 75 percent of the questions that test only recall

❏ Having the new questions reviewed for cognitive level by a learning professional with expertise in test design.

D4: Drive Learning Transfer

In the next eight weeks, I will pilot the use of an online learning transfer support system so that I can test its value in our programs and increase post-instruction transfer and application.

Indicators of my progress will include selection of the system and a completed plan for integrating learning transfer, including assessing its impact after the first pilot group.

D5: Deploy Performance Support

In the next eight weeks, I will create and implement a comprehensive plan to increase the engagement of participants' managers. It will include tips, forms, and timelines, as well as a letter of expectation from the relevant senior leader, so that managers of participants know that they are expected to coach their direct reports and are supported in doing so.

Indicators of my progress will include seeing a higher level of coaching reported by participants and feedback from managers about the coaching support's value.

D6: Document Results

In the next eight weeks, I will create an evaluation plan for the JKL Program that will produce relevant, credible, and compelling evidence of its business impact so that we can convincingly prove its value and also gather insight to improve it further.

Indicators of my progress will include developing the design and gaining buy-in from management that these are the right measures of success.

Amabile, T., & Kramer, S. (2011). *The progress principle: Using small wins to ignite joy, engagement, and creativity at work*. Boston: Harvard Business School Publishing.

American Express. (2007). The real ROI of leadership development: Comparing classroom vs. online vs. blended delivery. www.personneldecisions.com/uploadedfiles/Case_Studies/PDFs/AmericanExpress.pdf.

Anderson, J. (2010). *Cognitive psychology and its implications* (7th ed.). New York: Worth Publishers.

Ariely, D. (2010). *Predictably irrational: The hidden forces that shape our decisions*. New York: Harper.

Atkinson, T., & Davis, J. (2003). *Forum's principles of workplace learning: Insights and tools for performance improvement*. Boston: Forum Corp.

Babbie, E. (2010). *The practice of social research*. Belmont, CA: Wadsworth.

Basarab, D. (2011). *Predictive evaluation*. San Francisco: Berrett-Koehler.

Boehle, S. (2006). Are you too nice to train? *Training, 43*(8), 16–22.

Brafman, O., & Brafman, R. (2008). *Sway: The irresistible pull of irrational behavior*. New York: Doubleday.

Brethower, D., & Smalley, K. (1998). *Performance-based instruction: Linking training to business results*. San Francisco: Pfeiffer.

Brinkerhoff, R. (2006). *Telling training's story: Using the success case method to improve learning and performance.* San Francisco: Berrett-Koehler.

Brinkerhoff, R., & Gill, S. (1994). *The learning alliance: Systems thinking in human resource development*. San Francisco: Jossey-Bass.

Brinkerhoff, R., & Montesino, M. (1995). Partnerships for learning transfer: Lessons from a corporate study. *Human Resource Development Quarterly, 6*(3), 263–274.

Broad, M., & Newstrom, J. (1992). *Transfer of training: Action-packed strategies to ensure high payoff from training investments.* Cambridge, MA: Perseus Books.

Buzan, T. (1993). *The mind map book.* London: BBC Books.

Charan, R. (2001). *What the CEO wants you to know: How your company really works.* New York: Crown Business.

Clark, R.C. (2008). *Developing technical training: A structured approach for developing classroom and computer-based instructional materials.* San Francisco: Pfeiffer.

Clark, R.C. (2010). *Evidence-based training methods: A guide for training professionals.* Alexandria, VA: ASTD.

Clark, R.C., & Mayer, R. (2011). *e-Learning and the science of instruction: Proven guidelines for consumers and designers of multimedia learning* (3rd ed.). San Francisco: Pfeiffer.

Clark, R.C., Nguyen, F., & Sweller, J. (2006). *Efficiency in learning: Evidence-based guidelines to manage cognitive load.* San Francisco: Pfeiffer.

Colvin, G. (2006). What it takes to be great. *Fortune, 154*(9), 88–96.

Connolly, M., & Burnett, S. (2003). Hewlett-Packard takes the waste out of leadership. *Journal of Organizational Excellence, 22*(4), 49–59.

Dirksen, J. (2012). *Design for how people learn.* Berkeley, CA: New Riders.

Dulworth, M., & Bordonaro, F. (Eds.). (2005). *Corporate learning: Proven and practical guides for building a sustainable learning strategy.* San Francisco: Pfeiffer.

Ericsson, K., Prietula, M., & Cokely, E. (2007). The making of an expert. *Harvard Business Review, 85*(7/8), 114–121.

Feldstein, H., & Boothman, T. (1997). Success factors in technology training. In J.J. Phillips & M.L. Broad (Eds.), *Transferring learning to the workplace* (pp. 19–33). Alexandria, VA: ASTD.

Gawande, A. (2009). *The checklist manifesto.* New York: Metropolitan Books.

George, M. (2003). *Lean six sigma for service: How to use lean speed and six sigma quality to improve services and transactions.* New York: McGraw-Hill.

Harburg, F. (2004). They're buying holes, not shovels. *Chief Learning Officer, 3*(3), 21.

Heath, C., & Heath, D. (2008). *Made to stick: Why some ideas survive and others die.* New York: Random House.

Holton III, E. (2003). What's really wrong: Diagnosis for learning transfer system change. In E. Holton III & T. Baldwin (Eds.), *Improving learning transfer in organizations* (pp. 59–79). San Francisco: Jossey-Bass.

Holton III, E., Bates, R., & Ruona, W. (2000). Development of a generalized learning transfer system inventory. *Human Resource Development Quarterly, 11*(4), 333–360.

Islam, K. (2006). *Developing and measuring training the six sigma way: A business approach to training and development.* San Francisco: Pfeiffer.

Jefferson, A., Pollock, R., & Wick, C. (2009). *Getting your money's worth from training and development.* San Francisco: Pfeiffer.

Kahneman, D. (2011). *Thinking fast and slow.* New York: Farrar, Straus and Giroux.

Keller, J. (1999). Motivational systems. In H. Stolovitch, & E. Keeps (Eds.), *Handbook of human performance technology,* (2nd ed.). San Francisco: Jossey-Bass.

Kelley, H. (1950). The warm-cold variable in first impressions of persons. *Journal of Personality, 18*(4), 431–439.

Kerfoot, B., & Brotschi, E. (2009). Online spaced education to teach urology to medical students: A multi-institutional randomized trial. *American Journal of Surgery, 197*(1), 89–95.

Kirkpatrick, D. L. (1998). *Evaluating training programs: The four levels* (2nd ed.). San Francisco: Berrett-Koehler.

Kirkpatrick, D.L., & Kirkpatrick, J.D. (2005). *Transferring learning to behavior: Using the four levels to improve performance.* San Francisco: Berrett-Koehler.

Knowles, M., Holton III, E., & Swanson, R. (2005). *The adult learner* (6th ed.). Burlington, MA: Elsevier.

Kotler, P. (1999). *Kotler on marketing: How to create, win, and dominate markets.* New York: The Free Press.

Kouzes, J.M., & Posner, B.Z. (2007). *The leadership challenge* (4th ed.). San Francisco: Jossey-Bass.

Langley, G., Moen, R., Nolan, K., Nolan, T., Norman, C., & Provost, L. (2009). *The improvement guide: A practical approach to enhancing organizational performance* (2nd ed.). San Francisco: Jossey-Bass.

Leimbach, M., & Emde, E. (2011, December). The 80/20 rule for learning transfer. *Chief Learning Officer*.

Mager, R., & Pipe, P. (1997). *Analyzing performance problems, or, you really oughta wanna* (3rd ed.). Atlanta, GA: CEP Press.

Maister, D., Green, C., & Galford, R. (2000). *The trusted advisor*. New York: The Free Press.

Margolis, F., & Bell, C. (1986). *Instructing for results*. San Diego, CA: University Associates.

National Research Council. (2000). *How people learn: Brain, mind, experience, and school*. Washington, DC: National Academy Press.

Neves, D., & Anderson, J. (2003). Knowledge compilation: Mechanisms for the automation of cognitive skills. In J.R. Anderson (Ed.), *Cognitive skills and their acquisition* (pp. 57–84). Mahwah, NJ: Lawrence Erlbaum Associates.

Patterson, K., Grenny, J., Maxfield, D., McMillan, R., & Switzler, A. (2008). *Influencer: The power to change anything*. New York: McGraw-Hill.

Pfeffer, J., & Sutton, R. (1999). *The knowing-doing gap*. Boston: Harvard Business School Press.

Pink, D. (2006). *A whole new mind*. New York: Riverhead Books.

Pink, D. (2009). *Drive: The surprising truth about what motivates us*. New York: Penguin Group.

Pollock, R., & Jefferson, A. (2012). Ensuring learning transfer. *Info-line*, 1208. Alexandria, VA: ASTD.

Porter, M. (1985). *Competitive advantage: Creating and sustaining superior performance*. New York: The Free Press.

Qin, Y., Sohn, M., Anderson, J., et al. (2003). Predicting the practice effects on the blood oxygen level-dependent (BOLD) function of an MRI in a symbolic manipulation task. *Proceedings of the National Academy of Sciences, 100*, 4951–4956.

Ries, A., & Trout, J. (2001). *Positioning: The battle for your mind*. New York: McGraw-Hill.

Rosenbaum, S., & Williams, J. (2004). *Learning paths: Increase profits by reducing the time it takes employees to get up-to-speed*. San Francisco: Pfeiffer.

Rossett, A., & Schafer, L. (2007). *Job aids and performance support: Moving from knowledge in the classroom to knowledge everywhere*. San Francisco: Pfeiffer.

Rouiller, J., & Goldstein, I. (1993). The relationship between organizational transfer climate and positive transfer of training. *Human Resource Development Quarterly, 4*(4), 377–390.

Russ-Eft, D., & Preskill, H. (2009). *Evaluation in organizations: A systematic approach to enhancing learning, performance, and change* (2nd ed.). New York: Basic Books.

Salas, E., Tannenbaum, S., Kraiger, K., & Smith-Jentsch, K. (2012). The science of training and development in organizations: What matters in practice. *Psychological Science in the Public Interest, 13*(2), 74–101.

Sharkey, L. (2003). Leveraging HR: How to develop leaders in "real time." In M. Effron, R. Gandossy, & M. Goldsmith (Eds.), *Human resources in the 21st century* (pp. 67–78). San Francisco: Jossey-Bass.

Shrock, S., & Coscarelli, W. (2007). Measuring learning—Evaluating level II assessments within the eLearning Guild. In S. Wexler (Ed.), *Measuring success: Aligning learning success with business success* (pp. 155–164). Santa Rosa, CA: The eLearning Guild.

Smith, R. (2011). *Strategic learning alignment: Make training a powerful business partner.* Alexandria, VA: ASTD.

Stolovitch, H., & Keeps, E. (2004). *Training ain't performance.* Alexandria, VA: ASTD.

Sullivan, J. (2005). Measuring the impact of executive development. In J.F. Bolt (Ed.), *The future of executive development* (pp. 260–284). New York: Executive Development Associates.

Swanson, R. (2003). Transfer is just a symptom. The neglect of front-end analysis. In E. Holton III & T. Baldwin (Eds.), *Improving learning transfer in organizations* (pp. 119–137). San Francisco: Jossey-Bass.

Tenner, A., & DeToro, I. (1997). *Process redesign: The implementation guide for managers.* Reading, MA: Addison-Wesley.

Thull, J. (2010). *Mastering the complex sale* (2nd ed.). Hoboken, NJ: John Wiley & Sons.

van Adelsberg, D., & Trolley, E. (1999). *Running training like a business: Delivering unmistakable value* . San Francisco: Berrett-Koehler.

Vance, D. (2010). *The business of learning: How to manage corporate training to improve your bottom line.* Windsor, CO: Poudre River Press.

Vroom, V. (1995). *Work and motivation* (classic reprint). San Francisco: Jossey-Bass. (Originally published in 1964.)

Washburn, K. (2010). *The architecture of learning: Designing instruction for the learning brain.* Pelham, AL: Clerestory Press.

Wick, C., Pollock, R., & Jefferson, A. (2009). The new finish line for learning. *T & D, 63*(7), 64–69.

Wick, C., Pollock, R., & Jefferson, A. (2010). *The six disciplines of breakthrough learning: How to turn training and development into business results* (2nd ed.). San Francisco: Pfeiffer.

Contents of the Appendix

❏ Ideas into Action

❏ Answers to Fill-in-the-Blanks

❏ Checklists

❏ Flow Chart for Ensuring Training Should Be Part of the Solution

❏ Job Aid for the 6Ds Outcomes Planning Wheel™

❏ 6Ds Application Scorecard

❏ Transfer Climate Change Planner

❏ Kinds of Data, Examples, and Uses

❏ Mind Maps

❏ Goal Form

Ideas into Action

Actions to Improve D1

❏ Read the business or operating plans for the units you support.

❏ Attend business and operational reviews.

❏ Ask questions if you do not understand terms or concepts.

❏ Look for ways in which training and development can help address business issues.

❏ Review the programs for which you are responsible to be sure each has objectives that are credibly linked to business imperatives.

❏ Interview the business sponsor for a new or existing program using the Outcomes Planning Wheel. Triangulate the results with other stakeholders if appropriate. Summarize your findings and share with the key stakeholders.

❏ Create co-ownership of results by helping managers understand that training will fail unless it is accompanied by appropriate incentives, systems, and managerial support on the job.

❏ Review the incentive and performance review systems; if they are incompatible with the training, the training will fail. Call this to management's attention.

❏ Help managers find a more effective alternative when you can see that training is not the right solution.

❏ Complete the checklist for D1 (later in this Appendix).

Actions to Improve D2

❑ Review your course descriptions and invitations. Rewrite them if necessary to make the benefits and the value proposition clear.

❑ Review the pre-work you currently require. Is it essential? Is the amount reasonable? Does it truly add value for the time required? Take action to address any issues you discover.

❑ Maximize the probability of success by facilitating manager-participant interaction prior to training.

❑ Provide specific structure and guidelines for the meeting. Consider requiring a "learning contract" between the manager and his or her report.

❑ Develop specific plans that engage managers after training; they can make or break the success of any initiative.

❑ Redefine the finish line for training. Attach credit or certificates of completion to on-the-job application rather than simply attendance.

❑ "Staple yourself to a learner." That is, walk through the experience from the learner's perspective to make sure it is complete and coherent.

❑ Be vigilant for mixed messages—where what is taught in the program and what is practiced in the business are inconsistent. Such inconsistencies discourage participants from trying to transfer their knowledge and, if glaring, lead to cynicism.

❑ Complete the checklist for D2 in this Appendix.

Actions to Improve D3

❑ Review your program and calculate the amount of time learners sit passively being presented content versus the amount of time that they are actively engaged in applying the material. Adjust the ratio if necessary.

❑ Review a key program to make sure that the instructional methods and media are the best way to teach the required skills and behaviors.

❑ Test a program design (whether internally developed or from a vendor) by attempting to draw a value chain that links each topic and exercise to the required skills and business outcomes. Correct any disconnects.

❑ Compare the learning objectives to the business outcomes. Do they truly reflect the skills and knowledge needed to improve performance?

❑ Review the assessments used in your programs. Do they really measure the ability to *apply* new knowledge or skills, or merely to regurgitate minutiae?

❑ Obtain advanced training in writing reliable and valid assessments if this is not already an area of strength for you.

❑ Assess the extent to which participants understand the relevance, utility, and value of what they learned and whether they feel confident that they can use it in their work. Address any issues identified.

❑ Complete the checklist for D3 in this Appendix.

Actions to Improve D4

❑ Have a candid discussion with senior management about how the actions (or inaction) of participants' managers enhance or destroy the value of learning. Work with management to ensure that there is on-the-job support for learning transfer.

❑ Incorporate the transfer climate scorecard into planning for critical programs; engage business leaders in scoring it and discussing the results.

❑ Have each participant set specific goals or action plans for application. Send a copy to her or his manager.

❑ Remind participants periodically following training about the need to apply what they have learned.

❑ Stimulate reflection and recall by posing questions or circulating tips or additional information during the transfer period.

❑ Survey or interview participants in a recent, high-profile program to assess the level of managerial support for its application. Share the results with senior management.

❑ Provide managers with short, practical, specific actions they can take to enhance learning transfer.

❑ Complete the checklist for D4 in this Appendix.

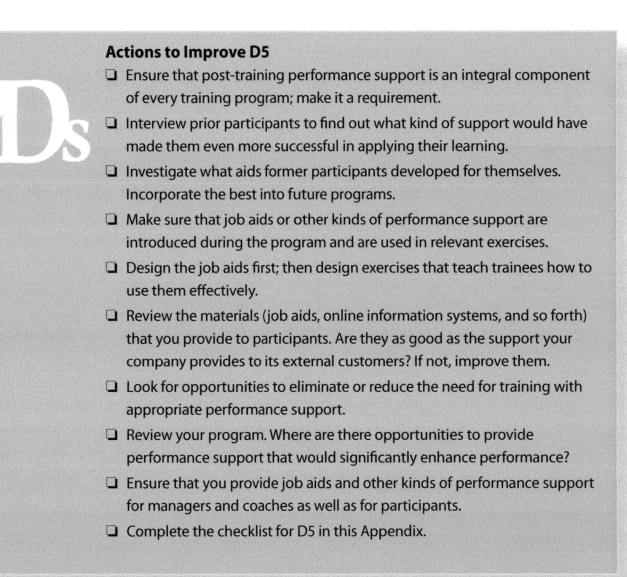

Actions to Improve D5

❑ Ensure that post-training performance support is an integral component of every training program; make it a requirement.

❑ Interview prior participants to find out what kind of support would have made them even more successful in applying their learning.

❑ Investigate what aids former participants developed for themselves. Incorporate the best into future programs.

❑ Make sure that job aids or other kinds of performance support are introduced during the program and are used in relevant exercises.

❑ Design the job aids first; then design exercises that teach trainees how to use them effectively.

❑ Review the materials (job aids, online information systems, and so forth) that you provide to participants. Are they as good as the support your company provides to its external customers? If not, improve them.

❑ Look for opportunities to eliminate or reduce the need for training with appropriate performance support.

❑ Review your program. Where are there opportunities to provide performance support that would significantly enhance performance?

❑ Ensure that you provide job aids and other kinds of performance support for managers and coaches as well as for participants.

❑ Complete the checklist for D5 in this Appendix.

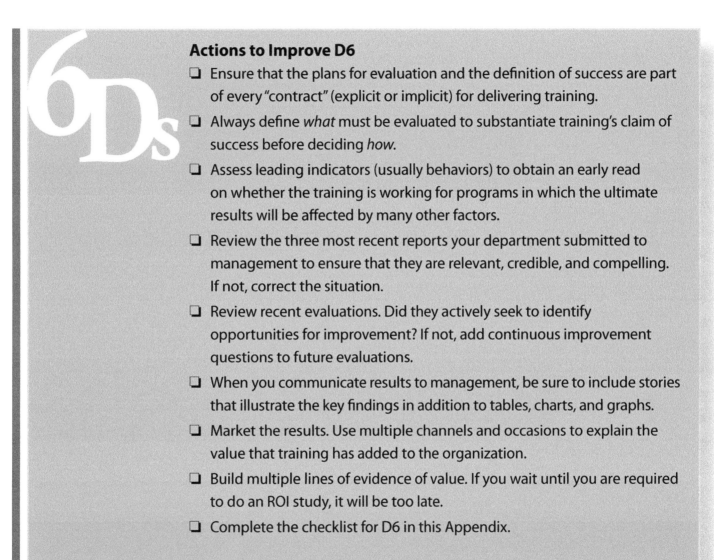

Actions to Improve D6

❏ Ensure that the plans for evaluation and the definition of success are part of every "contract" (explicit or implicit) for delivering training.

❏ Always define *what* must be evaluated to substantiate training's claim of success before deciding *how*.

❏ Assess leading indicators (usually behaviors) to obtain an early read on whether the training is working for programs in which the ultimate results will be affected by many other factors.

❏ Review the three most recent reports your department submitted to management to ensure that they are relevant, credible, and compelling. If not, correct the situation.

❏ Review recent evaluations. Did they actively seek to identify opportunities for improvement? If not, add continuous improvement questions to future evaluations.

❏ When you communicate results to management, be sure to include stories that illustrate the key findings in addition to tables, charts, and graphs.

❏ Market the results. Use multiple channels and occasions to explain the value that training has added to the organization.

❏ Build multiple lines of evidence of value. If you wait until you are required to do an ROI study, it will be too late.

❏ Complete the checklist for D6 in this Appendix.

Answers to Fill-in-the-Blanks

Introduction

Page	Answer

Page   **Answer**

4   1. Training's *product* is <u>improved performance</u>, not programs or modules; they are just the means to an end. Organizations "buy" training in the expectation of improved performance.

4   2. Our *value* to individuals and to the organization as a whole is the extent to which we help them <u>improve performance</u> and meet their <u>business objectives.</u>

13   When you receive a request for training—even if you strongly suspect that training is not an appropriate response—the first words out of your mouth should be: <u>"I can help you solve your problem."</u>

13   <u>"If their lives depended on it,</u> would <u>they still not be able to perform?"</u> (*Analyzing Performance Problems*, p. 93).

Which path an employee chooses depends on the answers to two fundamental questions (Figure I-6):

16, 17   ❏ <u>Can I?</u>

- <u>Did the program actually teach me how?</u>
- <u>Do I have the opportunity?</u>
- <u>Am I confident enough to try?</u>
- <u>Can I get help if I need it?</u>

❏ <u>Will I?</u>

- <u>Am I motivated enough to make the effort?</u>

- <u>Am I convinced it will help me?</u>
- <u>Will anybody notice if I do?</u>
- <u>What does my boss think?</u>
- <u>What do my peers think?</u>

D1: Define Business Outcomes

Page   *Answer*

30   Therefore, at the highest level of generalization, there are only two ways that training can contribute to success (Figure D1.1):

❑ <u>Increase income</u>

❑ <u>Decrease costs</u>

33   How would you describe its advantages compared to, say, "A cheap, tinny frame that is bolted together from a lot of pieces"? <u>Stronger, more crash-resistant, less likely to crumple on impact.</u>

34   Therefore, how would you explain the *benefits* of the one-piece frame to a potential car buyer? <u>Greater safety and peace of mind for you and your family.</u>

34   In general, what is the difference between a feature and a benefit? The difference is that features are <u>attributes of the product itself,</u> whereas benefits <u>explain the "what's in it for me"—the value of those features to the purchaser.</u>

	Traditional Learning Objectives	Business Outcome Objectives
Time Frame	End of class	On the job
Focus	Knowledge or capability	Actions and results

38

D2: Design the Complete Experience

Page   *Answer*

58   What the research showed: <u>even a random number influenced people's opinions.</u>

60   Participants in a training program generally fall into one of three groups:

1. <u>Prisoners</u> ("I am just here to serve my time.")
2. <u>Vacationers</u> ("This will be a nice break from real work.")
3. <u>Explorers</u> ("I am interested in learning something new or better.")

71   It implies <u>"you're done"</u> and it reinforces the prevailing paradigm that all you have to do is show up and you have fulfilled your obligations.

D3: Deliver for Application

Page   *Answer*

80   Two key themes run through this workshop:

1. Training is a means to an end; that end is <u>improved performance.</u>
2. Training produces improved results only when it is *applied* to the work of the individual and organization.

87   A discussion, problem to solve, case example, relevant game, and many other activities can afford meaningful practice, provided the exercise has the following characteristics:

❏ It mirrors the way the new information and skills <u>need to be used on the job.</u> Which is rarely, if ever, just regurgitating facts.
❏ It includes <u>meaningful feedback on performance.</u>

93   Where controlled trials have been done, the medium doesn't matter *as long as <u>the instructional method is the same</u>* (Clark, 2010, p. 50).

93   The problem with selecting the medium first is <u>not all media can support all instructional methods.</u>

97   A useful model for thinking about the motivation to apply new skills at work is Vroom's Expectancy Model (Figure D3.6), which says that effort is proportional to motivation and that motivation is driven by:

❏ <u>Expectancy: I believe this will help my performance.</u>
❏ <u>Instrumentality: I believe that improved performance will be rewarded.</u>
❏ <u>Valence: I value the reward.</u>

98   One of the key principles of adult learning is that adults want to know <u>why</u> they are being asked to learn something before they will do so willingly.

D4: Drive Learning Transfer

Page   *Answer*

113   Many manufacturing companies now routinely achieve Six Sigma quality: less than one defect per <u>300,000</u> units.

121   Why are the results so dramatic? Because at the low transfer rates typical of most training programs today, <u>most of the value goes unrealized, and so affords a rich target of opportunity</u> (Figure D4.3).

123   Identifying root causes means <u>looking behind the obvious, immediate causes</u> and getting to the real heart of the issue.

125   In process improvement terms, "low-hanging fruits" are issues that are <u>relatively easy to fix but which have a big payoff in terms of the improvement produced.</u>

125   Rouiller and Goldstein defined the learning transfer climate as: <u>all of the practices and procedures used in an organization that signal to people what is important.</u>

134   What lesson can we learn? If we want to keep the application of new skills and knowledge top-of-mind, then <u>we need to remind people periodically after training.</u>

135   There is solid learning theory behind this: Every time you retrieve information, you <u>strengthen the neural connections to it</u>, which makes it easier to recall and use in the future.

137   American Express concluded that: "an immediate leader has the potential to either <u>make or break</u> any training effort."

D5: Deploy Performance Support

Page   *Answer*

157   The goal of providing performance support is to *make certain that* <u>everyone does the right thing every time.</u>

161   Sometimes, the support that is needed can only come from a human being. Examples include:

❑ <u>Feedback on complex tasks like consulting or presentation skills</u>
❑ <u>Suggestions for how to improve a proposal or piece of writing</u>
❑ <u>Advice on handling a difficult employee or customer issue</u>
❑ <u>Expert troubleshooting skills for a technical or software issue</u>

165   "When the leadership teams share their development needs with each other and use the coaching model, they often find three things: (1) they have <u>similar issues</u>, (2) they get <u>great improvement suggestions</u> from each other, and (3) they get <u>support</u> from each other to improve" (Sharkey, 2003).

 D6: Document Results

Page   *Answer*

175   While it's useful to ask people at the end of training whether they feel prepared and motivated to use what they learn (see D3), that isn't sufficient because: <u>it does not predict whether they actually will use it; the transfer climate has a profound impact</u>.

178   ❑ If you reduced the cost of training by 25 percent by using more e-learning AND the effectiveness was the same or greater, then you deserve <u>a promotion</u>.

    ❑ However, if you reduced the cost by 25 percent but the effectiveness declined by 33 percent, then you deserve <u>something quite different</u>.

179   An effective evaluation is

    ❑ **<u>Relevant</u>** to the program's purpose
    ❑ **<u>Credible</u>** to the stakeholders
    ❑ **<u>Compelling</u>** to the decision-makers
    ❑ **<u>Efficient</u>** in its use of resources

183   *How* you would actually evaluate each claim requires:

         a.   An agreed-on definition and

         b.   A valid and reliable measurement instrument.

191   The only reason to measure anything is to inform action.

195   **IMPORTANT:** Don't bother trying to improve efficiency unless the other three criteria have been met. **Doing the wrong thing at low cost is not efficient!**

196   Evaluation should always serve to *prove* as well as to *improve* value creation.

197   More often than not, the real impediments to transfer are in the transfer climate, and that insight can only be gained by evaluating transfer after days or weeks back on the job.

■ Checklists

Overall (Preflight) Checklist for a New Program

D1: Define	☐	Program objectives are stated in terms of what the participants will do on the job following the coursework, as opposed to just what they will learn.
	☐	The criteria for success and how they could be measured have been discussed with the program sponsor(s).
	☐	Alternatives to training have been explored and rejected. Factors that affect performance *in addition to* training are included in the plan.
D2: Design	☐	A robust plan is in place for the pre-course period that includes educating managers regarding their role, a compelling invitation, and meaningful preparatory work for participants.
	☐	Post-instructional support, accountability, and recognition for learning transfer are included in the overall design.
D3: Deliver	☐	The relevance of each program element has been mapped to the overarching business objectives and will be clearly communicated to participants and their managers.
	☐	Material will be presented in ways that emphasize and facilitate its application. Adequate time is provided for participants to practice new knowledge and skills.

D4: Drive	☐	A system of accountability for learning transfer is in place. Participants are reminded periodically of the need to continue to practice what they learned.
	☐	The program is not considered complete until there is evidence of transfer to the employee's work. Improved performance is recognized and rewarded.
D5: Deploy	☐	The design includes post-course performance support: easily accessible content, tools, and advice to assist participants in putting their learning to work.
	☐	Systems and processes are in place to help participants engage coaches (peers, managers, experts, etc.) for feedback, advice, and support.
D6: Document	☐	The program design includes how the on-the-job results identified in D1 will be evaluated. The program sponsors have agreed, in advance, to the evaluation method, timing, measurements, and definition of success.
	☐	The evaluation plan includes collecting and analyzing data specifically to identify opportunities to improve the program's preparation, instruction, and post-course support.

Checklist for D1

❏ The proposed training addresses a performance issue related to lack of knowledge or skill.

❏ Non-training solutions have been explored or tried and rejected.

❏ Environmental factors that will affect successful implementation (such as incentives, consequences, coaching, etc.) have been identified and discussed.

❏ Objectives are clearly linked to high-priority, high-value business needs.

❏ Objectives state the actual performance that will be achieved (as opposed to knowledge, ability, or capability) and use business terms and concepts.

❏ Objectives clearly indicate how success could be measured and specify the performance standard to be met and by when.

Checklist for D2

❏ The invitation/course description is clear and compelling. It focuses on the benefits rather than just the features.

❏ There is meaningful preparatory work—reading, exercises, simulations, performance feedback, etc.—that will help maximize the time spent in the learning program itself.

❏ A pre-program meeting between the participant and his or her manager is strongly encouraged (ideally, required). Guidelines and worksheets for that meeting are provided.

❏ The instruction itself is designed to maximize application (see also Checklist for D3).

- Structure, support, and accountability for learning transfer are included in the program design (see also Checklist for D4).
- Post-instructional performance support is an integral part of the program design (see also Checklist for D5).
- The "finish line" for the program is defined weeks or months after the instruction. There is a plan in place to assess achievement and participants know what it is.
- There is a plan to ensure recognition for significant improvement and accomplishments as a result of applying the training.

Checklist for D3

- Program descriptions, materials, and instruction answer the "What's-in-it-for-me?" (WIIFM) question for participants.
- The links between the program content and the current business needs and job responsibilities are clearly stated and then reiterated for each major exercise or topic.
- Relevant examples, stories, simulations, discussions, and so forth are included to help learners see how the material applies to their jobs. Success stories from prior graduates of the program are used to underscore its utility.
- The preparatory work is utilized extensively in the program—so much so that those who did not complete it are at a disadvantage (or, ideally, are not allowed to attend).
- The agenda provides adequate time for learners to practice the desired skills or behaviors with supervision and feedback so that they can answer the "Can I?" question in the affirmative.
- Job aids are introduced during the instruction and used in exercises.

❏ The materials, equipment, situations, and settings are as close to the actual work environment as possible.

❏ Participants' perceptions of the program's relevance and utility are solicited, tracked, analyzed, and acted upon.

❏ Assessments gauge the learners' ability to apply the skills and concepts, not just recall them.

Checklist for D4

❏ Processes are in place to periodically remind participants of their obligation to apply their learning, hold them accountable, and recognize superior efforts and accomplishments.

❏ Participants and managers meet following the course. Managers are provided concise, specific, and practical guidelines for that meeting.

❏ Managers actively support the use of new skills and knowledge, help identify opportunities to apply new skills, set relevant goals, provide feedback, and help work through difficulties.

❏ Managers are reminded of the program's objectives and informed of their direct reports' personal goals for application, if appropriate.

❏ Job aids and specific guidance are provided to coaches and managers to help them fulfill their roles in facilitating learning transfer.

❏ Senior management recognizes the importance of managerial support and recognizes and rewards managers who do a superior job of developing their direct reports.

❏ Appropriate recognition is planned for trainees who make great progress and/or complete their objectives.

Checklist for D5

❏ Performance support is an integral part of the design; difficulties or memory lapses that trainees might encounter are anticipated and addressed.

❏ Learners are provided with job aids, online materials, apps, help desks, and so forth to help ensure they are successful when trying new skills and behaviors.

❏ Continued learning and peer-to-peer sharing after the formal instruction period is encouraged and facilitated.

❏ Learners are provided easy and efficient ways to engage their managers, subject-matter experts, instructors, or other advisors during the transfer and application process.

❏ Former participants are polled to discover what additional support would have helped them; aids they have developed for themselves are solicited and incorporated in future programs.

Checklist for D6

❏ The ways in which the program will be evaluated have been discussed and agreed on with the program's sponsor(s) in advance.

❏ The proposed evaluation meets the guiding principles of efficiently generating relevant, credible, and compelling results.

❏ The earliest (leading) indicators that the program is working have been identified. A plan is in place to use these as in-process checks to drive improvement during the roll-out.

❏ The sources of the data that will be used in the evaluation have been identified; their availability has been confirmed. A plan is in place to gather needed data that are not already collected routinely.

❑ Consideration has been given to what the post-training results will be compared with to make the claim of "better," "improved," and so forth.

❑ Assistance from the finance department has been secured if the sponsor has defined financial analysis of the return on investment as a criterion for success.

❑ The evaluation plan actively seeks out information to identify opportunities for improvement of subsequent programs.

❑ The evaluation plan has been reviewed by someone "skilled in the art" for validity and reliability.

❑ How the data will be reported and presented has been considered; the key audiences for the results have been identified and there is a communications plan for each.

Flow Chart for Ensuring Training Should Be Part of the Solution

Could they do it correctly if they absolutely had to (if their lives depended on it)?	
NO	**YES**
Training is probably part of the solution. Probe to understand what kind of training and what other changes are needed to ensure success.	RED FLAG! Training is unlikely to solve the problem. Try to help the manager identify and correct the real impediments to performance (see below).
This suggests that a lack of knowledge or skill is a contributing factor and that training is appropriate. Gain additional insight by asking: Is this a completely new process, information, or skill? • If yes, then plan and execute the training using the 6Ds. Can they barely manage the task, or aren't very proficient? • Focus on practice with feedback. Could they do it in the past, but they have forgotten or are rusty? • Plan a refresher with a focus on practice and coaching. Do they just need information? • Consider other ways to supply the information rather than "training." Would a good job aid suffice? • If so, provide it to free limited training resources for where they are needed more.	If people could perform as expected, but are not, then the real problem is the "Will I?" question. Try to get to the root cause by asking: Are employees clear about what is expected of them? • If not, clarify. Have they received unambiguous feedback on their current performance? • If not, see that they receive it. Is there any reward or recognition for performing in the desired fashion? • If not, see that there is. Are there any negative consequences for not performing as expected? • If not, make sure there are. Is something else getting in the way, such as inadequate time or resources, overly complicated process, managerial indifference, etc.? • If so, fix these; training won't work in an unhealthy transfer climate.

Job Aid for the 6Ds Outcomes Planning Wheel™

Use this job aid to help you achieve the greatest value from using the 6Ds Outcomes Planning Wheel in your discussions with business sponsors and stakeholders.

Preparation

Do your homework. Read relevant plans or other documents beforehand. Think about what you want to accomplish and how you want to structure the conversation. Business leaders are busy people; make efficient use of their time and stick to the time frame agreed on.

Opening

How you open the discussion with business leaders is important, especially as the approach you are going to take may be different from what they have been used to in the past. Use a consultative approach to open the conversation:

- ❏ **Meet and greet**
- ❏ **State the value:** "I am here today because we want the training we design for you to deliver real business impact and value. Training takes time and costs money. The better I understand your business needs and the outcomes you are looking for, the more value we can deliver for you."
- ❏ **Propose an agenda:** "I'd like to ask you a few questions to clarify the business needs you want this training to meet, the kinds of changes we need to produce, and how we will know whether the program is achieving its goals. I understand we have scheduled ___ minutes for this meeting."
- ❏ **Check for agreement:** "Is the agenda OK? Anything else you want to be sure we cover?"

RESULTS:
Workshops are a success if 90% of participants improve skills post-training, and a majority of managers agree meetings are more efficient and less painful.

GOALS:
Save time and improve decision making by improving presentation skills to be clear and efficient.

MEASURES:
Progress will be confirmed by improved presentation scores by observers from communication dept. Time savings on surveys by senior management.

BEHAVIORS:
Clearly state purpose first. Follow clear & logical structure. Make clear recommendations. Support with analysis and solid facts. Avoid death by PowerPoint.

Seek Understanding

Many business leaders are used to simply "ordering" some training to address a perceived need. They may not have thought deeply about the questions at the heart of the 6Ds Outcomes Planning Wheel. You may need to ask some probing or clarifying questions to achieve the level of understanding required to develop a truly effective program. Some comments and suggested follow-up questions are given below.

Throughout the conversation, practice active listening. Stop and check for understanding periodically: "Let me be sure that I have correctly understood. [Restate the needs, behaviors, etc., as you understand them.] Is that correct?"

Do not be afraid to admit you do not understand something. Ask: "Could you explain what you mean by. . . ." Another very useful phrase is: "Help me understand. . . ." This phrase can be used to genuinely seek understanding. It is also a graceful way to point out inconsistencies or confusion: "Help me understand how the training course you have requested is linked to your business needs."

Using the Four Outcomes Planning Wheel Questions
1. What business need(s) will be met by this training?
Your goal is to clarify what the person requesting training is trying to accomplish in business terms.

GOALS

1. What business needs will be met?

Situation	Suggested Response
If the first answer is too general, for example, "increase sales," probe for the intermediate steps/behaviors needed.	*I understand that the critical need is to increase sales. Can you help me understand the intermediate steps? What are the specific behaviors that contribute to increased sales that we need to address in this training?*

If the first answer is too narrow, for example, "We need to use the order entry system better," probe for the ultimate, measurable outcome.	*I understand the immediate need is to improve the use of the order entry system. What is the ultimate goal? For example, fewer errors? Lower cost? Greater speed?*

2. What will participants do differently and better?

BEHAVIORS

2. What will participants do differently & better?

People have to do things differently to obtain a different result. Just "knowing" or "understanding" is not enough to improve performance. Your goal is to understand what trainees are supposed to *do* as a result of the training.

Situation	Suggested Response
If the first answer describes what learners will know or understand, ask for desired changes in behavior.	*If the training is a success and we were to watch how people act afterward, what would we see them doing that is different and more effective?*
If the manager struggles to describe desired changes in behavior, ask how the better performers behave.	*Can you give me some examples of what the better performers do that lesser performers don't?* *Presumably, the training should help more people do what the better performers do. What would that look like?*
If the manager seems to hope that training alone is going to create the desired changes in behavior, help him or her understand that training is almost never the whole answer.	*In addition to the training, what needs to be in place to support and encourage these behaviors, such as incentives, consequences, managerial reinforcement, etc.? What might get in the way of people behaving in the desired fashion? How could we reduce or eliminate these impediments?*

MEASURES

3. What or who could confirm these changes?

RESULTS

4. What are all the specific criteria of success?

3. What or who could confirm these changes?

Your goal here is to identify ways to assess the effectiveness of the training and transfer climate.

Situation	Suggested Response
If the manager is not sure how to respond or is stuck, explain that, if the training works, it should produce an observable change in actions, perceptions, or business metrics.	*If we achieve the desired changes in the learners' behaviors, who will notice the changes?* *Do we have any systems or measures already in place that will change if we obtain the desired results? If so, what are they and how will they change if the training is successful?*
If the first answers describe large-scale or long-term effects that will be difficult to tie to the training itself (for example "retention will improve"), probe for immediate effects and leading indicators.	*I can certainly understand that that is the long-term goal, but it will take quite a while to show up, and it may be hard to figure out whether it was the training or something else that caused it. What would we see more immediately that would indicate that the training is working?*

4. What are your specific criteria for success?

Your goal is to gain agreement in advance on how the sponsor defines success. That is, how much of a change is necessary for the sponsor to feel the investment was worthwhile? As with SMART business objectives, the measures of success should specify *how much by when*. This is the time to establish whether or not the sponsor requires financial analysis of the return on investment, and if so, what he or she considers acceptable evidence of ROI.

Situation	Suggested Response
If the answer is "Give me an example," then provide suggestions based on the answers you have received to the first three questions.	*For example, if 50 percent or more of a sample of customers report that they feel the representatives are doing a better job of responding to their needs than in the past, would that be sufficient evidence that the program is having an effect?*
If the manager suggests an overly broad or too-long-term measure—for example "See if turnover goes down"—then try to get closer to an immediate impact of the program.	*I understand that—ultimately—higher retention is the goal. But that will take a long time to show up and will be influenced by many other factors. Since we know retention is linked to employee satisfaction, would you agree that the program is working if, ten weeks after training, a majority of direct reports of the attendees rate them as more effective?*
If the manager is still struggling to define success, try asking a different way.	*Perhaps this will help: Imagine it is four months from now and we meet in the hall. You say to me: "That training program was the best investment I made this year." What would have to be true for you to say that?*

Follow-Up

It is very important that you check your understanding and confirm the agreement in a follow-up memo after the meeting. Thank the person you interviewed and briefly summarize what you heard. This memorandum of understanding will give the interviewee a chance to correct any oversights or misunderstandings and will be a useful reference throughout the planning process.

A suggested format for the follow-up memo is given below:

Date:

Subject: Summary of Our Discussion

Dear _____:

Thank you for taking the time yesterday to meet with me to discuss your training needs.
I am writing to confirm my understanding of the business drivers and criteria for success.

The underlying business need that this program is designed to address is _____
_____.

If the training is a success, then the trainees will do (more/less) of _____ and
_____ in their work.

These changes will be evident to _____ and will be measured by _____
_____.

To ensure these actions and behaviors, the following steps need to be taken by their managers:
_____; and the following changes need to be made in
the work environment: _____.

The program will be considered a success if _____.

Please let me know if I have correctly summarized our discussion so that we can work together to
maximize the return on this training investment.

Sincerely,

6Ds Application Scorecard

Use this tool to evaluate the readiness of a program to deliver results and identify strengths on which to build as well as opportunities for improvement. For each item, check the box that best describes the program using the following key:

        0 = Not at all

        1 = To a small extent

        2 = Somewhat

        3 = To a large extent

        4 = To a very great extent

		0	1	2	3	4
Define	1. The business needs are well understood. Anticipated on-the-job results of the training are clearly defined and measurable.	❑	❑	❑	❑	❑
	2. Course objectives are communicated to participants and managers in terms of expected business impact.	❑	❑	❑	❑	❑
Design	3. The pre-instruction preparation phase is an integral part of the design. Meetings with managers are facilitated. Pre-work is fully utilized during exercises and instruction.	❑	❑	❑	❑	❑
	4. The training is considered complete only when there is evidence of successful transfer and application on the job.	❑	❑	❑	❑	❑

Deliver	5.	The cognitive load of the program is manageable; there is sufficient time for practice with feedback for participants to develop proficiency.	❑	❑	❑	❑	❑
	6.	Each topic and exercise has a clear "line of sight" to required behaviors and business results. Participants' perceptions of the program's utility and relevance are monitored and acted upon.	❑	❑	❑	❑	❑
Drive	7.	After the program, participants are periodically reminded of their learning in ways that encourage reflection, retention, and application.	❑	❑	❑	❑	❑
	8.	Participants' managers are actively engaged during the post-training period. They monitor and actively support application on the job.	❑	❑	❑	❑	❑
Deploy	9.	Performance support is an integral part of the design. Participants are provided job aids, expert help, coaching, and other support as needed to facilitate transfer.	❑	❑	❑	❑	❑
	10.	Participants continue to learn from each other after the program. Peer coaching and sharing of best practices are facilitated.	❑	❑	❑	❑	❑
Document	11.	On-the-job actions and results are evaluated based on the business outcomes agreed to by the sponsor prior to the program.	❑	❑	❑	❑	❑
	12.	Information to support continuous improvement of the preparation, instruction, and learning transfer is actively solicited, analyzed, and acted upon.	❑	❑	❑	❑	❑

Transfer Climate Improvement Planner

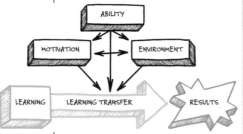

Factor	Actions to Consider to Improve Transfer Climate
Learner Readiness	• Be sure the course descriptions and invitations explain the benefits and expectations of the training. • Establish criteria or prerequisites for attendance to make sure the right people are in the room.
Opportunity to Use	• As part of the analysis, make sure that employees will have the necessary resources to perform as taught. • Insofar as possible, provide "just-in-time" training, so that trainees have the opportunity to use it soon afterward.
Personal Capacity	• Pay attention to how much change is being expected of employees; a new training initiative launched in the midst of a major reorganization is unlikely to succeed.
Perceived Relevance and Utility	• Monitor the perceived relevance and utility of courses and address low scores promptly. • Make the relevance of the training as a whole, and the individual exercises, clear. • Use equipment, materials, and circumstances that are as close to actual job performance as possible.
Motivation	• Provide examples of how prior participants have benefited. • Ensure that rewards and recognition are in alignment with what is being taught.

Organizational Culture	• Evaluate the extent to which the current culture supports or impedes new behaviors. • Share your insights with senior management; changing culture is a long-term and difficult project that they must lead.
Managerial Alignment	• Ensure managerial buy-in by seeking their input into the selection and prioritization of training programs. • Provide managers with job aids to help them set expectations in advance of training.
Managerial Encouragement	• Provide managers with short, specific, and practical things they can do to support learning transfer—including scripts if appropriate. • Provide training on coaching if necessary.
Managerial Feedback and Coaching	• Answer the WIIFM question for managers by showing them the evidence on how much additional value their coaching can create for their departments. • Provide short, specific, and practical guides for coaching for maximum performance.
Peer Group Impact	• Train intact teams so that the whole work group is exposed to the new methods simultaneously. • Offer incentives for team as well as individual performance.
Personal Experience	• Ensure that the performance appraisal and incentives systems are in line with what is taught in training rather than working against them. • Gain agreement with managers beforehand on the importance of both positive consequences for using the training, as well as negative consequences for allowing it to go to waste.

Kinds of Data, Examples, and Uses

Kinds of Data	Examples	Uses
Business Metrics	• Sales • Production statistics • Quality index • Number of complaints, accidents, incidents, etc.	To demonstrate and quantify specific business impact. To improve credibility as they are company records, although they are often difficult to link directly to training.
Observations	Customers', managers', co-workers', or trained observers' observations of • Sales technique • Presentations • Following procedure • Phone interactions	To demonstrate that the training, plus performance support, is changing behaviors on the job. Usually a leading indicator of business impact. In many cases, such observations are sufficient to meet the sponsor's criteria for success. Use rubrics to increase reliability.
Evaluation of Work Product	Expert evaluation of the quality of a work product such as: • Software code • Business writing • Strategic or marketing plan • Financial analysis	Before and after comparisons of work products can demonstrate that the training and support have improved the quality of the output. Consider using coded samples, rubrics, and/or external evaluators to increase the credibility and objectivity of the evaluation.

Kinds of Data	Examples	Uses
Opinions	People's perceptions of the quality of interactions or service such as: • Customer satisfaction • Leadership effectiveness • Teamwork • Clarity of communication	In some cases, for example, efforts to improve customer satisfaction or leadership effectiveness, opinions are the most relevant outcomes. Usually collected by survey or interviews. Care must be taken to avoid bias, for example, by ensuring anonymity.
Stories	• Stories explaining how learning was used successfully • Critical incidents • Lessons learned • Specific examples of application	Extremely useful for providing specific examples of on-the-job application to buttress other measures. A way to measure the transfer rate. Also useful for marketing the value of the program to future participants. Be sure to verify any story you use for this purpose.
Estimates	• Time saved • Frequency of use • Number of people (employees, customers) affected • Financial impact	Estimates will sometimes suffice when precise measures are not obtainable. To improve credibility, ensure that those making the estimates have an informed opinion and have no vested interest in manipulating them.

Mind Maps

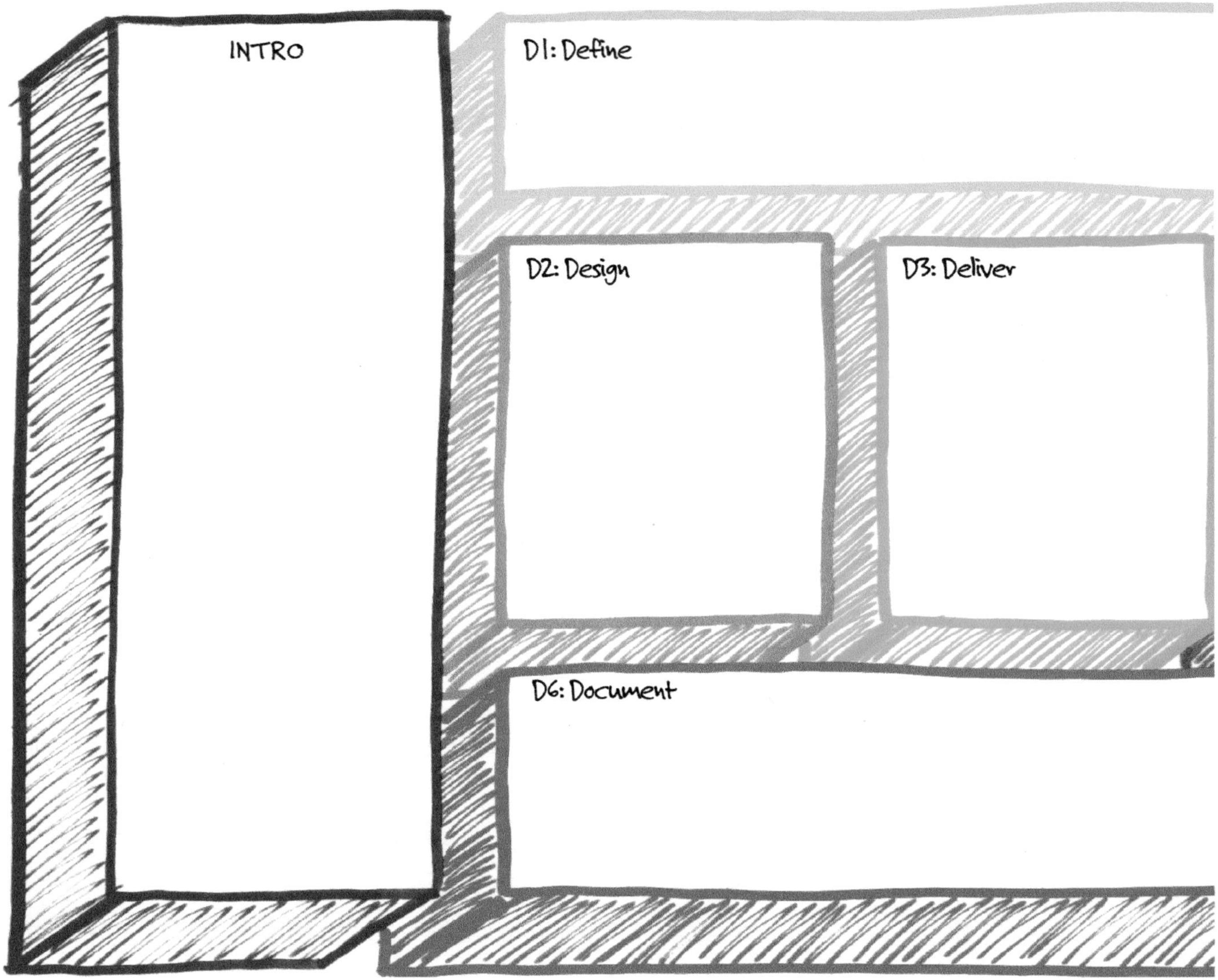

Figure A.1. Road Map to Results

D4: Drive

D5: Deploy

Figure A.2. Two Questions Mind Map

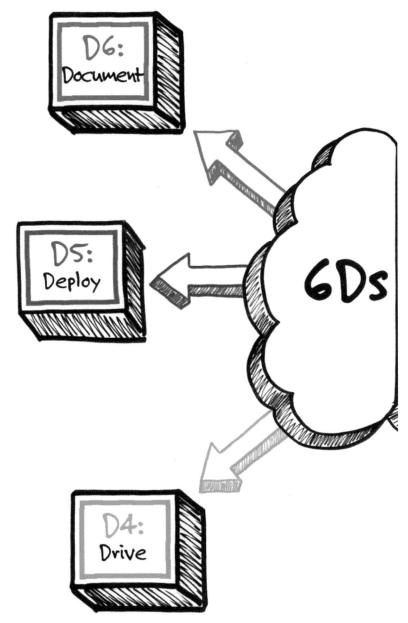

Figure A.3. 6Ds Mind Map

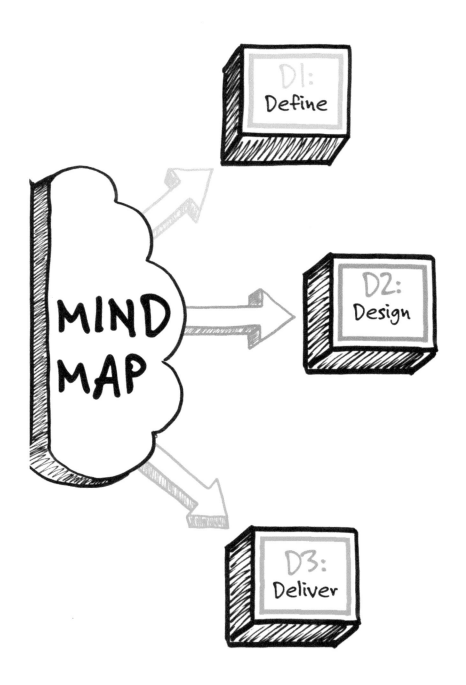

Roy V.H. Pollock, **DVM, PhD**, is Chief Learning Officer of The 6Ds Company and co-author of *The Six Disciplines of Breakthrough Learning* and of *Getting Your Money's Worth from Training and Development*. Roy has a passion for helping individuals and teams succeed. He is a popular speaker and frequent consultant on improving the value created by training and development.

Roy has a unique blend of experience in both business and education. He has served as chief learning officer for the Fort Hill Company; vice president, global strategic product development for SmithKline Beecham Animal Health; vice president, Companion Animal Division for Pfizer; and assistant dean for curriculum at Cornell's Veterinary College.

Roy received his BA from Williams College *cum laude* and his doctor of veterinary medicine and PhD degrees from Cornell University. He studied medical education at the University of Illinois. Roy has received numerous awards, including the Ralston-Purina Research Award. He is a Fellow of the Kellogg Foundation National Leadership Program.

Andrew Jefferson, JD, is President and Chief Executive Officer for The 6Ds Company. He is a co-author of *The Six Disciplines of Breakthrough Learning* and of *Getting Your Money's Worth from Training and Development.*

Andy is a frequent and popular presenter and consultant who excels in helping companies maximize the value they realize from their investments in learning and development. An accomplished executive, he has deep line-management expertise as well as experience in strategic planning, sales and marketing, enhancing productivity, and technology development.

Andy views learning as a critical source of competitive advantage in an increasingly knowledge-based economy. He knows first-hand the challenges of running a company and making every investment count. Prior to joining The 6Ds Company, Andy served as the chief executive officer of The Fort Hill Company, CEO of Vital Home Services, and chief operating officer and general counsel of AmeriStar Technologies, Inc.

Andy is a graduate of the University of Delaware and graduated *Phi Kappa Phi* with honors from the Widener University School of Law, where he served on the school's board of overseers.

Calhoun W. Wick, MBA, is the Chairman and Founder of the Fort Hill Company and co-author of *The Six Disciplines of Breakthrough Learning*. Cal is internationally recognized for his work on improving the performance of managers and organizations. In 2006, he was named "Thought Leader of the Year" by ISA, the Association of Learning Providers.

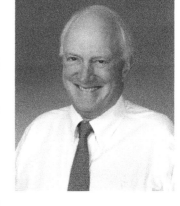

Cal recognized that the finish line for learning and development programs is no longer the last day of class; a trainee has completed a program only when improved performance has been achieved.

Cal earned his master's degree as an Alfred P. Sloan Fellow at MIT's Sloan School of Management.

About the 6Ds Company

The

The 6Ds Company was created to help companies achieve even greater returns on their investments in training and development through application of the 6Ds. We offer both open-enrollment and in-company workshops as well as consulting services. Additional information is available on our website: www.the6Ds.com or by writing info@the6Ds.com.

6Ds Workshop Goal Form

Please complete and turn in this goal form to the facilitator before you leave. It is an important part of the complete learning experience for this workshop.

PLEASE PRINT CLEARLY.

Your name: _____

Your email address: _____

Your manager's name: _____

Your manager's email address: _____

YOUR GOAL

In the next eight weeks, I will [describe what you will accomplish]:

So that [describe the benefit]:

Evidence of my progress will include [How will you know that you have made progress or achieved the goal?]: